Also by Charles Olson

Call Me Ishmael: A Study of Melville (1947)
Y and X (1950)
In Cold Hell, in Thicket (1953)
The Mayan Letters (1953)
The Maximus Poems / 1-10 (1953)
The Maximus Poems / 11-22 (1956)
Projective Verse (1959)
The Maximus Poems (1960)
The Distances (1960)
The Human Universe and Other Essays (1964)
A Bibliography on America for Ed Dorn (1964)
Proprioception (1965)
Gedichte (1965)
Charles Olson Reading at Berkeley (1966)
Selected Writings (1967)
The Maximus Poems IV, V, VI (1968)
Causal Mythology (1969)
The Special View of History (1970)
Archaeologist of Morning (1970)
Letters for Origin, 1950-1956 (1970)
Poetry and Truth (1971)
Additional Prose (1974)
The Post Office (1975)
The Maximus Poems: Volume Three (1975)
Charles Olson & Ezra Pound: An Encounter at St. Elizabeths (1975)
The Fiery Hunt & other plays (1977)
Muthologos, I and II (1978, 1979)
Charles Olson & Robert Creeley: The Complete Correspondence. Vols. 1-8
    (1980-1987)
The Maximus Poems (1983)
The Collected Poems (1987)
Charles Olson & Cid Corman: Complete Correspondence. 1950-1964,
    Vol. 1 (1987)

CHARLES OLSON

A NATION OF NOTHING BUT POETRY

SUPPLEMENTARY POEMS

EDITED BY GEORGE F. BUTTERICK

BLACK SPARROW PRESS   SANTA ROSA   1989

LIBRARY OF CONGRESS CATALOGING-IN-PUBLICATION DATA

Olson, Charles. 1910-1970.
   A nation of nothing but poetry : supplementary poems / Charles Olson : edited by
     George F. Butterick.
   p.   cm.
  Includes index.
  ISBN 0-87685-751-9 : — ISBN 0-87685-750-0 (pbk.) : — ISBN 0-87685-752-7 (deluxe) :
  I. Butterick, George F. II. Title.
PS3529.L655N38   1989
811'.54—dc19   88-36879
                                                               CIP

Contents

INTRODUCTION

THE University of California Press *Collected Poems of Charles Olson,* published in 1987, is at 700 pages long enough, and even that format necessitated the exclusion of much valuable work, including useful variants and extensive notes. This volume consists of poems omitted from that collection, including alternate versions of poems published there, with distinct and instructive differences. Most others are wholly new, never published before in any form. Choices had to be made in compiling the previous volume.

There were not only the usual limits of the economics of publishing, but also the consideration of an economy of means, a recognition of the effect of redundancy on even a devoted audience. Nothing is gained heaping up the evidence, overwhelming the reader. Too many poems at once diffuses the poet's accomplishment. It was desirable to avoid intimidation and ponderousness (as it is, some will find the 700 pages of *The Collected Poems* ponderous enough). Publishing everything is no solution to the authority problem, the situation that exists when there is no longer a living author to guide us.

At the same time, tastes change; they differ. Judgment is at best relative, or at least rarely eternal. Students of poetry and of Olson's work specifically, might welcome the chance to compare significant variant texts. There is, as William Carlos Williams observed, no end to desire. As long as some of these texts don't distract, this volume can be all gain.

Only five of the hundred and ten poems have been published before in these versions: "Lost Aboard U.S.S. 'Growler,'" "For K.," "To Corrado Cagli," "Name-Day Night," and the eight lines beginning "Oh! fa-doo: the enormous success of clerks," which had been sent to Robert Kelly anonymously or perhaps actually signed, as it appears in the magazine *Matter,* "an anonymous contributor from Wyoming, New York." Several of the others—like many of the early poems in *The Collected Poems*—had been sent out by Olson for publication, without avail. "Birth's Obituary," for example, was rejected by the *Partisan Review,* "1492–1942" was turned down by both the *Sewanee Review* and *Virginia Quarterly,* and "Idle

Idyll'' was rejected by Raymond Souster for his *Contact*.

The editor's notes following the poems give a fairly detailed indication of the considerations used to date these poems, which are presented in chronological order. From these notes it will also be seen that the poet's latest version was not always the one included in *The Collected Poems*. The latest is not always the best, as Olson himself provides the model of, in returning to his original version of "I, Maximus of Gloucester, to You" for the 1960 *Maximus Poems*.*

There are still as many as two hundred, perhaps, non-*Maximus* poems and fragments remaining behind among Olson's papers, but they are for another sensibility or another age. I have exhausted my intelligence. I cannot imagine they would benefit most readers or contribute to the poet's reputation. But this is my judgment; let others refine or redefine his corpus as they will. The important thing is that the present generation have the present texts, in all their variety, for whatever use might be made of them.

All sorts of uses can be made of them. The tribute to Ford Madox Ford, "Auctour," reminds us of Olson's links to the older generation. "The Moon" becomes "The Moon Is the Number 18" (*CP*, 201). "Who it is who sits . . ." situates "The Babe" (*CP*, 101) more clearly between "La Préface" (*CP*, 46) and both "The Kingfishers" and "The Praises" (*CP*, , 86 and 96). "Lady Mimosa" is yet another flowering of "The She Bear" (*CP*, 129). "I met my Angel last night . . ." and its alternate (*CP*, 586) are two versions of the same dream. In "Melville's sense of blooming late . . ." we have the author of *Call Me Ishmael* still caring about Melville thirty-seven years after first reading *Moby-Dick*.

I have tried to include only poems with *significant* differences from their other versions. The difference between variants usually goes beyond mere line arrangement, although that too can alter a poem's specific effect. In a number of cases, other versions that are merely useful for purposes of comparison remain behind among the poet's papers, where specialists can consult them. The deciding factor in presenting these texts is that they have

---

*See my *Editing the Maximus Poems* (Storrs, 1983), p. 5.

value in their own right. And if they throw light on another version, that too is a welcome result.

One brief example of the process of editing as selecting might be offered. Because of the exigencies of space and because the poem itself is not a crucial Olson poem — the way that "La Préface" is, or the first ten poems in the *O'Ryan* series — the version of "Examples — for Richard Bridgeman" (*CP*, 555) titled "Apoptic" was omitted from *The Collected Poems*. It is also, perhaps, a somewhat atypical Olson poem, apparently meant to be an exercise or encounter whose subject is language, the American language itself, dedicated to the author of "The Stylization of Vernacular Elements . . ." (then being rewritten into *The Colloquial Style in America*) and intending to display as *much* language as possible. In "Apoptic," there is the language of speech, the language of reference, repossessed and reinvented language, language as pun, the sheer arbitrariness of "otors," language to its near-Latin roots, private vs. public, real vs. surreal language, rapid-eye-movement language, language as flight simulator traveling from one terrain of consciousness to another, literally crash-landing language. As Olson said at Goddard College a few days later, "One of the boring things about most writing in America is slang. . . . Our cultural speech is a form of slang . . . It's like dialect. I hate it." (Surprising, at first, coming from Olson, although he means slang which is derivative and self-conscious even though all slang is.) In any case he goes on: "I myself would wish that all who spoke and wrote, spoke always from a place that is *new* at that moment that they do speak . . ." (transcribed from the Goddard tape, 12 April 1962, Goddard College Learning Aids Center).

"Examples" and "Apoptic," then, have never been spoken before, even by the Olson of the *O'Ryan* series. They are completely fresh, completely invented, spoken "from a place that is *new* at that moment that they do speak." Between the two versions, however, one is as good as another. It was the closest I had to come to making an arbitrary decision regarding *The Collected Poems*, choosing the version I did. Before making that choice, I tried every means known to me to determine a preferred or "superior" or even a later version, without success. In the original typescript of "Apoptic," on the conveniently erasable

Racerase bond, there are remnants of a word under "violent" in the last line. I was hoping it was "violet," as in "Examples," which would then indicate that Olson has stopped, erased the "n," and returned to type "violet" as his ultimate choice. But it was not to be. Now, at least, the reader can share both possibilities.

Readers can make up their own minds. In some cases among the variants, a single line or stanza alone may be preferable to the corresponding passage in the "definitive" version. The title, "The Gleeman Who Flattered You," for instance, might be preferred to the more quaintly self-conscious "Thy Gleeman Who Flattered Thee" (*CP,* 514) — even though "thy" and "thee" are consistent with "gleeman," or medieval minstrel and also more appropriate to head a poem written with Gloucester inventor and medieval enthusiast, John Hays Hammond, Jr., in mind. In that case, however, one then loses "sleep / will be so coldly built you'll / scratch like those drowned sailors / mewing outside the telephonic hull . . ." It is not a simple decision, but through this volume the reader can share it.

This, then, is a supplement, a complement, to the University of California Press's *Collected Poems.* It is not meant to compete with that edition for primacy. Neither is it intended to be an introduction to one of the most important and complex poets of recent times. Nor is it a sampling of neglected highlights from Olson's poetic career. These are simply poems, which by themselves possess integrity and interest so that they ought to be made available as well.

Of the previously unpublished poems and versions, all but a handful are from among the poet's extensive papers housed in the Literary Archives at the Babbidge Library, University of Connecticut. The few others (those not previously published) were scouted out from other public repositories or individual recipients of the original manuscripts. I would like to thank Robert Creeley, Kenneth McRobbie, and Washington University Libraries, St. Louis (Holly Hall and Timothy Murray) in this regard. And, for providing information useful for dating the poems or in preparing the notes, I wish to acknowledge the kindness of Richard Bridgman; Monroe Engel; G. Thomas Tanselle of the Guggenheim Foundation; Lilly Library, Indiana

University (Saundra Taylor); Frank L. Moore; the Newberry Library, Chicago (Carolyn A. Sheehy); Olin Library, Wesleyan University (Elizabeth Swaim); and Simon Fraser University Library (Percilla Groves).

George F. Butterick

A NATION OF NOTHING BUT POETRY:
SUPPLEMENTARY POEMS

❋ Birth's Obituary ❦

Plane's flight your helix, transcontinental blood
Of Indian girl, fledged by the modern,
New Archeopteryx, you Hart Crane
Flew where others falter.

I remember your death, and reject all answers.
Noon, high time, at Orizaba stern you stood.
In ecstasy of wake you who made a bridge leaped!
Span made act, your death another Myth propelled.

Space, our shroud and swaddle, makes each a navigator.
Cathay lies where we must go, and if you end
In channel as another did in chains,
Oh Hart, wave-right you are!

You drank the poison as Crockett the cloud,
Man of large thirst. Now you drink
The golden goblet of the sun
The silver chalice of the moon.

✳ "Atalanta ran swift course . . . ✳

Atalanta ran swift course
The inward tender of her foot
fire upon my source

Leda lay beside the sea,
made Michelangelo of me

        Your dryad eyes, your naiad arms
        ended the body of a boy's alarms.

Sweet willow of desire!
Eurydice!
O wife twice lost!
Your body's white song of my lyre

        Stone and spear
        Bend and fall from my ear

❀ Mavrodaphne ❀

White horse he was to her black foal.
Behold! they were desire.
They woo'd, but 'gainst a world in shoal
Feared their fire.

He grew more human,
Less woman she.
Image approached
Animality.

With grace he asked
Return to world;
Reply and hate,
To a tree she curled.

A man and a tree
No marriage be.
She sought another,
Became a mother—
What of the three?

❀ Conqueror ❀

I met a Worm,
He turned on me.
I cried:
He died.

❋ Crown of Nails ❋

The nail of the Cross
Bit of Constantine's horse
  — Action was bred,
    The body bled,
    Motion was dead.

            Man can live by bread alone,
            Flesh be no crone,
            Not the Divine in man
            But the Man in man
            The Dream be known.

     Who can speak
     When, in the throat,
     Angels squeak?

     What image shall float
     When, at ship's peak,
     Waves Christ's coat?

Cross and Charger beat man down
But Blood again shall be man's crown.
That "fabulous formless darkness" raise
Before the Past and the Dream's amaze.

❋ Mindanao [1] ❋

Where you are deep
I am
in seed's leap
found

Naked diver
dove
in blue
and found no pearl
but you!

Returned to day
my eyes stay
dark
and see.

❋ Mindanao [2] ❋

Where you are deep
I am
in seed's leap
found

Naked diver
dove
in blue
and found no pearl
but you!

Returned to day
my eyes stay
dark
and see
that verity!

❋ No ❋

No. The foot of me
shall step no step
bone muscle nerve
do not propel.
I will be slow.

No. Nor mind shall lead
where obdurate flesh
fat with future to be past
refuse to follow.
Mark me slow.

Slow. Sight and act
as stubborn as earth
as quick as bud
alone are mine.
I shall say no.

❋ Raphael ❋

Last night I heard
Raphael had
A concept of negation.
But when did concept
Ever lead to creation?
When God conceived
Was He deceived
And took it for negation?
When Adam delved and Eve span
And made us all a nation
Was that
—negation?

❋ Sea Song ❋

Heave the net
To catch the being,
Draw the net
To heave again.

Heave the net —
Shark and minnow
Whale and perch —
Heave again!

Torn is your net.
In your nakedness
Someone comes!
Leap overboard!

The kraken no man ever saws in blue night of bottom.

Mend your net,
On green fields
Spread it out
To sun the tar.

Gather the net,
Breathe sun and salt,
Go to sea,
Heave again!

Porpoise and monk,
Fin and scale,
Whale and minnow,
Heave!

❋ Who Sings Against Things ❋

Lie next to the wall
At night fall
For love is all,
For love is all.

Men will answer
Arms, and the strike's call,
But love is all.
Lie next to the wall.
Love is all.

Events intrude,
Break solitude.
But under night
Beside the wall
Love is all.

In crush of worlds
Man swirls.
His day is death.
But draw the breath
At night fall
Next to the wall
love is all,
love is all!

❋ Capricorn ❋

Capricorn of mountain thirst
drank the waters of the First
ancient Aquarius poured

Awaiting the Bull and Spring,
bored he watched the Fishes' leap
and the Ram run

After love
the Twins divided him
opposing the Sea his father
to goat-Mother land

With Summer he took his motion
sideways as the Crab
to find the Virgin and the Lion
his marriage with the Sun

Last quarter like the moon
brought dark.
In the Weigh of doubt
The Sting of fear
the Centaur's arrow in the loins
he who had mounted the Year
ascended again the Peak of his birth

❋ Lustrum ❋

So, Pound, you have found the gallows
you, with your fingers at your nose
and in your mouth the laugh, dirty or otherwise

They'll cant your body, canto maker.
Sudden, and your neck freckled red
will break as broke some others', nameless
—all but Booth—in the gray Washington snow
after another treachery, another war

Or do they shoot you now
And will it be a new thing here
to be a poet after you are broken?
Because they did not know the Pound
they killed was also Pound the poet

Or did they, and you were the prize of the lot
the Villon of their peace, the thing
they are always after, in day out
o enemy of the happy ending.

What the hell did you broadcast for?
Did you have to be historic, Yorick?
Mug the mike with your ABCs
you even made Galway Willie sneeze:
revolutionary simpleton.
Ezra Pound, American

Who pays? These are not the great days.
No hunt, sir, and what you take for bays,
Propertius, are the rattle of cans
We who are younger here
could have helped you there:
This is a time to survive, exile

O Pound, forgive us, for shall we die
of better things than syphilis and treason

when we are old and blind:
your Heine left his mattress grave
and missed the bullets in the Rue de Slave
to have a look at Venus nate
in '48
and now it's you, another way
unblind and gay
lover of the obscene
by the obscene undone

fecit, Pound, fecit

❋ Lost Aboard U.S.S. "Growler" ❋

Black at that depth
turn, golden boy no more
white bone to bone, turn
hear who bore you weep
hear him who made you
deep there on ocean's floor
turn, as waters stir, turn
bone of man

Cold, as a planet is
cold, beat of blood no more
the salt sea's course
along the bone jaw white
stir, boy, stir
motion without motion
stir, and hear
their love come down

Down as you fell
sidewise, stair to green stair
without breath, down
the tumble of ocean
to find you, bone
cold and new among the ships
and men and fish askew

You alone o golden boy no more
turn now and sleep
washed white by water
sleep in your black deep
by water out of which man came
to find his legs, arms, love, pain

Sleep, boy, sleep
in older arms than hers
rocked by an older father;
toss no more, son
sleep

❊ My Father ❊

My father was my father
but my mother was the moon
She I have but he
died too soon

So I must be my father
— double up —
and catch all things
in one silver cup

He used to sing
he used to play
he used to hammer
and walk all day

She made me young
she made me gay
she made me turn
the other way

He used to whistle
he used to laugh
he had to do both
— he dare not cry —
he was a calf
and very shy

I liked his heart
I liked his eye
I liked his sense
of the other guy

He had a smell
he had a breath
he was sweet
death, you cheat

I had a father
he died too soon
I am lonely
me and my moon

❋ 1492–1942 ❋

Grip space
aces and eights
elbow room
you rate:
where air?

Grab earth
six feet
the wide open
go west
big shot:
who love?

Drag the sea
fathom five
kicker diesel
steel trawl
highline:
what sun?

when?

❋ Winter ❋

bitter winter

rain
rain down, all moving things
Blind, with care as under-
ground go by each
Turned in
as claws (across the day)
curled in their dark, intent
Go. Where?
     will rain
     does the sun
     will rain put out
     does the sun know
     will rain put out the fire,
     the bitter fire?

winter wind,
city wind,
enters the bones
(as fear comes)
blows down as men move
weak
the next corner colder than the bones are cold
cold, yet when the fire comes
the wind will make
     will the wind
     the fire higher
     will the wind be left
     or the heat be too much for the wind and the
       rain?

wet snow
the wet street slow to let it gather
(as men the death ahead)
it falls as night exists
inhabiting itself

32

falls, whitens roof, pavement, ground
and if men stir. . . .

       or do the ashes also burn
       when men ignite the nitrogen of air?

❋ She, Thus ❋

The bottom of the air is disturbed
as with an undertow
Breathing is difficult,
and though the winds blow
Heaviness is upon me.

  His strictures tighten, bind my wonder
  Cramp the questions of my flesh.
  And the thunder of his voice!
  Huddle-muddle in my ear.

  I cannot recapture the play I need,
  the run and nonny of a sun and sea.
  I am too quick for his slow pace.
  The flight of my blood, Atalanta race
  Guys his deliberate course.

  He drops gold apples. I stop, admire.
  Something he fails to do hurts like wire.

  Intent, a bird, I ask if this be love.
  Turtle-wise, he knows, appetite on move.

  I work and, inside, prick myself, a needle.
  I waste, and call myself a weed, a nettle.
  Yet know I am as lovely as a flower,
  as subtle as the image in the pool,
  a queen of love, fashioned for misrule.

In the meadow where he wooed me on that rock I caught.

  I look back and there, apt, he comes.
  I lose my step: where are the other ones?
  He does not seem to run the faster
  And yet, I do not know, he is the master.

O make the wind blow sweeter
O make the air be light
For I would have my breath again
And be your love tonight!

❋ For K. ❋

Sex the sword. If not so armed
A man will hide within himself.
The armed man too, but battle
Is an outside thing, the field
Its own reward, reality.

Who fights behind a shield
Is separate, weak of the world,
Is whirled by sons of self sown
As teeth, a full armed crop
Sprung from no dream
No givers of a fleece
Who bring their dragon blood inside,
Reality, half slain.

    Join sword and shield, yield
    Neither ground, contend
    And with one stroke behead
    The three, the enemy

    Then, like a Greek, emboss
    The shield with legs, and boast
    Of mighty ancestry

✣ For A. K., Enniscorthy, Keene, Virginia ✣

1

The trees John Coles planted
More than a hundred years ago
Are bare in the winter wind
Where they are not jointed
With this week's snow

2

He chose this ridge of hunting green
When he came up the James
He cut the timber, turned the earth
Had crops, bore children, learned

The fall of the land was a part of dream
And when he looked for names
He thought of Ireland, remembered birth
Built, had fire, his first son burned

3

Coles, and now a Kulikowski live
Upon this land, within this tragic house

Holly without, linden, maple, oak
A yew to say lives end when others thrive

Below the barns the fearful gully yawns
Dark, the trees gigantic stalagmites

Reach up, a cave of forest growth he
Who first came here, was frightened of
And turned his back upon, paleozoic night

The light is all in front, south, east, west
The dry lot and the road ahead, the fruit trees east
And west the fields for barley, lespidesa, wheat

4

The house he built of brick and wood
The "office" down below
Stand out against the northern sky
Are sharp, with winter, spare
As was his Enniscorthy
Those hundred years ago

✸ Auctour ❧

Said Man of Hate, in lated tribute to Good Huffer:
"In gratitude for, your Grace and dispensations
I weep coarse thanks, of the living to the dead"

Said Pound the Red, one turquoise earring at his head
"FMF knew more than any of us, he . . . .
from the literary centre, 12 years start of me"

Say I: the Dropsical Man, with beauté in his eye
An Ancient thing, some lumped Raftery
To play the Heart at court of a King

The Dressing Gown, with breath behind the word.
Himself his acre, green island in the modern sea.
Presiding on Fifth Ave. — with new Les Amis.

O Generous Crotchet, with song along the prose
O Fifth Queen Crowned — with a cup of tea:

a writinge man in his lone glorye

✺ Of Love ✺

Of Love, defunctive music, the turtle-dove.

From the woods, of the long afternoon, the first note
The up-cry, Tur-tle, the caught breath
The hurt, as if an arrow struck the throat.

The comment then, the three repeats, of plaintive key
Low
Dove dove dove
The loss
The death of love.

❋ Ladies and Gentlemen, the Center Ring! ❦

1

The legs of Lalage toss, and toss, and toss
l'esprit de femme
against the canvas of a circus sky.

2

LE GRAND PLANGE, her own, the eighty turns,
in her native tongue, technically known thus:
Einigearmerisenschwunge. Look!

3

The legs of Lalage toss, and toss, and toss
l'hommage de l'homme
Lie open as they turn, play
On the bed of air, stir lazy in the whirl
As though she dreamed, curl to make short thigh
Whip, move:
This PLANGE the new gratuity.

4

Lalage! Lalage! her legs une porte aux bras
Her arm une pointe, her act le grand tourner
Her swing: inverted fouetté
On stage of revolutionary night.

5

Or call her Lalagea, and go back
To Horace, and the image of his love

And sing, rond en rond, as time does turn
As she turns, high, by single arm and ring
Sing: Lalage, Lalage, the legs of Lalage!

6

Sing: Lalage, Lalage, the legs of Lalage
Toss, and toss, and toss, l'esprit de femme
Across le cirque, le rêve de l'homme.

❋ Lalage ❋

1

> Haie! Lalage!
> the legs of (haie!)
> Lalage!

"To you, o rigid king, Lalage presents"
postures
in the circus sky
(metropolis! look, your thyrsus! high!)
asking, make trial and see
do not I present reality?

> Ai-ee! the legs
> high toss the legs
> (ai-ee!) Lalage!

I turn (regard me, amulet)
twisting, twisting, frenzy-stung
from a ring my one arm giant swing
I fling, I fling
in the face of you — once rigid king!

> Yi-ee! Lalage!

2

The legs of
whip, and whip, whip
lie open as they turn, play
on bed of air, go straight, snap shut, curl
to make short thigh, stir
(as though she dreamed, Bromios!)
her body's plange what's left —
this lady isolate

                    this gratuity
                    —what's left, Bromios

3

She climbed the brazen heaven,
the rope (your image) wooed to make her mount.
With hands and arms, at first. Then, stair by stair,
her body jack-knifes, quick, snap, a stripper's snare
until, at height to celebrate her rite, she sits
alone, o king, at ease on air, her spotlight altar, you
twisted around her ankle, held
sure between her thigh

4

Yes, Lalage: bacchante.
What's left, bacchante.
"High-tossed let the wild wands swing"
evoe

You, clamour-king no king, regard.
(Avoid! avoid!) Regard Lalage:
her one arm female giant swing
throwing, throwing the legs of
the unmanned legs of

                    Lalage!
                    the legs of
                    (sparagmos!)
                    Lalage!

❊ The Way of the Word ❊

The way of the AUSPEX:
by artifice to absolute

of HARUSPEX:
by lightning and entrail

:

   the actual bird, to the word

❋ The Moon ❋

The MOON is a monstrance

       the blue dogs bay.
       A spiky host,
       the blue dogs cry.

       In the moon
       the man
       grins.

       In the tower
       a cat and a crab sit
       to watch the face of the water, and fire.

       The blue dogs paw,
       lick the droppings
       dew, or blood
       night the crab rayed round
       attentive as the cat
       to catch man's sound.

       The blue dogs rue as men do
       as men do howl
       striate the snow
       as forms of flame the dark.

       In the red tower
       in that tower
       where the man sits
       the mad give
       birth.

Birth is an instance as is a host, namely, death.
The moon has no air.

The MOON is the number 18.

❋ To Corrado Cagli ❋

Upon a Moebius strip I saw
materials and the weights of pain, their harmony
Pull down thy head, o man

I saw a man pulled up, turned from me
hunched within himself upon an empty ground.
His head at first lay heavy on a huge right hand
itself a pad, a weight of head, a leopard on
his left and angled shoulder;
his back a stave, his side a hole into an awing bosom of a
    sphere.
And as he sat locked in this illness and this fear
and as his head passed down his sky (as suns the circle of
    the year)
his other shoulder, open side, and thigh
by law of conservation of
the center of his gravity maintained
their clockwise place in his descent
(the seventh, nth dimension of his turn
this turning sore, this blazing round)
until he knew, until he came to apogee
and earned and wore the moon as amulet.

I saw another man lift up a woman in his arms
he helmeted, she naked too, protected only as Lucrece by
    her alarms.
Her weight tore down his right and muscled thigh
but they in turn returned upon the left
to carry violence its outcome in her eye.
It was his shoulder that sustained, the right,
bunched as by buttocks or by breasts,
and gave to each the wildness of their rape.

And three or four who danced,
so joined as triple-thighed and bowed and arrowed folk
who spilled their pleasure once as yoke
upon a Grecian plain.

47

Their bare and lovely bodies sweep, in round
of viscera, of legs
of turned-out hip and glance, bound
each to other, nested eggs
of elements in trance.

❋ X to Zebra ❋

for F.Z.M.

Steorra, stir
by the bird's whir

    we are mixed
    here in the middle place
    choked in event

The tresor is hid.
Dig. I want a fool

    to bury the hanged man

and two women to put their hand on him
(neither one a papess)
to tell a fact when they see one.
Actually there are two, and they know it,
a quantity and a gout.

The answer to Grave's disease is
the grave, the question
have you enough chaos in you, man,
to make a world? (A.E. to Joyce, a Dublin street, 1910)

(C.O. to C.C., Second Ave., spring, 1946):
Sir, it's a wicked pack of stars you have!

✵ Willie Francis and the Electric Chair ✵

O Willie Francis didn't burn
When he sat in the electric chair
O Willie Francis didn't burn
When the current was on in the electric chair

Now the preacher told Willie
When he said his last prayer
"You're a lucky fella, Willie
To be goin' to the chair!"

    O Willie Francis didn't burn
    When he sat down in that big chair

Said the preacher to Willie
When he was going to fry
"Most don' know, and some ain't ready
But you is lucky, for you know you goin' to die"

    O Willie didn't burn, O Willie didn't burn
    When the good Lawd arranged it to be Willie's turn

Now the last word the preacher said
When Willie set out on the walk to the dead
"There are those who get squashed by trucks on the road
And those who die between sheets in their bed

    "O Willie," said he, "you're a lucky fella,
    You is goin' to know when you turn that black color."

Now they walked sad Willie into the room
It was shiny and clean as a new store broom
They sat down Willie right up in the air
And Willie knowed it was a bad chair

He tried to remember what the preacher had said
He tried not to think he'd just be dead.

It was just one thing: not how his hair'd be curled
But, "Willie you're goin out'a this world"

    O Willie didn't burn in that bad chair
    When they turned on the current he didn't turn a hair!

They strapped him in against the chair
And everything looked dazey in the air
The white folks watchin' seemed in a big swing
Away back they'd go, and then they'd swing in

    O Willie was in, O Willie was in
    He was goin' to pay for his big sin!

Now Willie breathed out and Willie breathed in
The white folks swung, and swung back in
And when they swung they swung up close
And Willie could hear their breaths in his nose

    O Willie was in, O Willie was in
    The white folks was makin' him pay for his sin

Now Willie had been to the picture show
He'd seen men drown, and otherwise done in
But he learned one thing as he sat in the chair
He didn't see his life in a flash sittin' there

    O Willie, O Willie had one thought there
    "You're goin' out'a this world in this bad chair"

Sometimes he thought it so loud that it hurt
And when they put his head in the big black bag
It hurt and it hurt, and his head was a rag
All locked up in the big black bag.

    O Willie was in with the loud thinkin'
    In the black bag for his black sin

    O Willie was in, O Willie was in
    In the black bag with the loud thinkin'

II

Now some folks say that dyin' is gold
And some folks say it's hominy grits
But Willie's been close and he oughter know
He says it's black, not gold or snow

> O Willie's been close, and he oughter know
> He says it's black and that oughter go!

The electric man said "Goodbye" to Willie
Jus' as tho' he were puttin' him on a bus to the city
And the way he said it, Willie tried to reply
But he couldn't get a word out no matter how he try

> O Willie, O Willie, o don't you try
> For the good Lawd's arranged it that you won't die

His mouth felt full of cold peanut butter
He couldn't say "Goodbye," he couldn't even mutter
The electric man stood by and Willie tried to answer
But his tongue got stuck in the peanut butter

> O Willie, O Willie, o don't you try
> For the good Lawd's arranged it that you won't die

Willie sat straight and Willie sat still
He says that chair makes you "plum mizzuble."
O Willie sat straight, and Willie sat still
He says that chair makes you "plum mizzuble."

Now the moment came when the switch was thrown
And there was Willie all on his own
He took it straight and he took it still
That he lived through it was the good Lawd's will

> O Willie sat in that big, bad chair
> And when they threw the current he didn't turn a hair

He felt a burning in his head
He felt his left leg go like red
His lips puffed out and he rocked the chair
But he didn't fry as he sat there

O Willie didn't fry, O Willie didn't fry
So all you people, don' you cry

He jammed his feet against the floor
As he went right up to death's big door
He jumped against the straps, they swore
To prove that Willie needn't burn once more

O Willie didn't burn, O Willie didn't burn
When the good Lawd arranged it to be Willie's turn

He said he saw a lot of lights
Blue and pink and little green speckles
The kind that shine in a rooster's tail
When he greets the morning from the nearest rail

O Willie didn't fail, O Willie didn't fail
When he saw the speckles on the rooster's tail

The preacher asked, "Did it tickle like I said?"
Willie said, "Yes, but it hurt in the head"
O Willie didn't die, O Willie didn't die
He's alive to hear the rooster cry!

"O electric man, o cut me free
The straps they are a cuttin' me!
O lectric man, o let me breathe
This big black bag is smotherin' me!"

O Willie didn't fry, O Willie didn't fry
He's goin' to live to say "Goodbye"

III

They cut Willie Free, they took him to court
The electric man said the current was short
And now they've gone to the big, big bench
To decide if the preacher saw Willie blanch

 O Willie are you free, O Willie are you free
 It's what the ten good men now shall see

When Willie was asked what he do if free
He said he would a preacher be
But if he gets life a cook he'll be
And serve sidemeat in the penitentiary

 O Willie be free, O Willie be free
 The best damned cook in the penitentiary

 O Willie is free, O Willie is free
 The biggest miracle in the whole country!

✳ "Adamo! Adamo! . . ." ✳

"Adamo! Adamo! something has harmed Adamo!"
went the cry, and the women weep, helpless
as he sits, listless, propped against a tree

"Adamo! Adamo! something has hurt Adamo!"
goes the cry, and the men stand, helpless
As Adam rests, listless, his head against the tree

"Adamo! Adamo!" moan the women, "Adamo!"
the day no day, no action, nothing done
the sun already red, but Adam! Adam down!

"Adamo! Adamo!" mumble his sons, "Adamo!"
questioning him, in questioning him to ask
if he decline do we not too decline?

That unbegotten day. The light had come
removed the night, the sun had dried the earth
but Adam did not speak, command, adore

"Adamo, speak! Father, say! the night!
how did the night undo you, what, what
deranged sweet morning, made you strange?"
                    makes you pine

❋ Your Witness ❦

name Pound, Ezra   born Montana   1887

journalist. As I see it history of today
literature is that stays news

. . a poem here and there. The live man
in a modern city feels this sort of thing or
perceives it as the savage perceives in the forest

I guess so yes if you mean a crank is
any man ANY other ambition save that of
saving his own skin from the tanners

I think the American system *de jure*
Adams Jefferson VAN BUREN
is probably quite good enough if
only 500 men (save that) with guts
the sense to USE it
or even with the capacity for
answering letters or
printing a paper

. . one should respect intelligence

. . another war without glory, another peace without quiet

The real life in regular verse is an irregular
movement underneath. Jefferson
thought the formal features of the American system
would work, and they did work till the time of Grant
but the condition of their working was that there
should be a *de facto* government composed
of sincere men willing the national good

. . the centre holds by attraction

I offer the hypothesis that: When a single mind
sufficiently ahead of the mass a one-party
system is bound to *occur as actuality* whatever
the details of form in administration

The CIVIL WAR drove everything out of the American
    mind.
Perhaps the worst bit of damage was it drove out
of mind the first serious anti-slavery candidate
not because he was an anti-slavery candidate but
because he saved the nation and freed the American
treasury

Well, if I ain't worth more alive than dead, that's that

. . that private gain is not prosperity, but that
the treasure of a nation is its equity

If a man isn't willing to take some risk for his opinion,
either his opinions are no good or he's no good

A good government is one that operates according to the
    best
that is known and thought. And the best
government is that which translates the best
thought most speedily into action

19 years on this case/first case. I have set down part of

. . stand with the lovers of

ORDER

❋ À Mirko, Knoedler, 1948 ❋

Elements of clothes, an arm
the hand   the head of a cock
turning, a cube and torso tour en l'air
a fish, free, the milieu man
facts, facts, fable et couleur

A crowd in a forest of the city make
attention turned as
the green republic, now renewed

The mount of the mass
objects as feathers piled
holds
the shining scales of space

the point a claw

✸ Stravinsky ✸

An Homage

On the edge of woods
(as we are)
the advance, retreat
of both
man as nature, nature as more than man
the sounds
tempi
fable
struggle-borne

On the edge of man
a horn   a hooded step (a stumble)   an echo led
by two white ropes
to this levitican point

On the edge
tympanum   and unicorn   telluric cube
he the balance
And the scale, the hounds:
man, and the maiden, both
torn

❋ Northman, What of Yourself? ❋

The buoy tosseth in the sea, it tolls
the waves causeth the bell to clang.
In the night my present people walk
the street I lived on as a child.

Tosseth the present in the past.
Two assume my parents' roles,
yet the play I clap-claw (audience, tool)
is a young man, aged out, title: fool.

The past causeth the present woe.
I meet myself on the familiar street.
She saws the air, he wears the hat he wore.
I swim among the split planks for the shore.

It is a play within a play, I sit front row
but too far right to see the action, know.
Was it the stage lip interfered?
Or was it canvas blocked my view,
and animals who played the parts
moved on and off through runs with prod and whip

In any case I missed
the meaning of the show.

❀ From *Troilus* ❦

Love is not present now, has flown
is not a state so separate as we think
that men and women breed by kiss and glance
no dance outside the modes and figures of that trance,
the full intent

That love at least must live
is lie we practice to protect
what we inherit, breath
unwilling to admit
the large wrongs bring
that also down to death
sour death

Why should love live
when all that should enforce it fails
this side of meaning? tears off
what it alone is key to, form
that feature nature wore, matter wore, Cressid
wore when matter stayed where objects are
when objects were our handles

when objects are, nature is, Cressid was
when Cressid was intact o! then, delight!
delight was still a possibility, delight
a round of human year, o! Cressid, my delight!
turn, turn, hear!

Love is not love with end, with objects lost.
Means wither. Bodies, gestures, fall   All Nature falls!
And on the path, are blown along the path, papers, dust,
    cloth
(strips which give no clue, dropped without care
picked up, lamely, at a dare)

The path, love is the path   And, in the forest, calls!

hear calls! which we shall, answer,
find

But if love now is lust, or mere drift back
better we know, and say,
                              we do know the way

The way, love is
the way!

❋ Name-Day Night ❦

(for James Stathes, George Pistolas,
and Stephanos Radis)

What it is to look into a human eye

men men what they are
who, of a sudden of a night in a room
a room not so different from this in which I sit
(along the floor circles of lamp light intersect),
start up, join hands, a kerchief joins them, their eyes follow
the pattern of their leader's feet their order,
they dance

what it is   what it is to say wherein it lies

where beauty lies
                    that men containeth
                                        at this hour

Came 2 a.m. the three men sang
one led (as in the dance) he of Peloponnesus
he sang of love, a narrative of man and maid
their meeting   what the youth said
the night left out the morning, final stanza, key

then proudly (as he had danced) the Macedonian
he sang of war most hieratically; Turks defeated
and, at each turning of the song, pistols shot off

None sang of death. I marked then, and ask now
what light it is shines in their eyes, what source
their gusto hath
this name-day night these men of Greece disclose
their eyes shine from outside, take light, shine
from nature, partake her common force, shine
by addition, separation, what is cruel

are not monocular, shine
by death its recognition, multiply
by life its shortcoming, shine
these eyes of night their sons and daughters know not of

And the hour tells what it is
                    what delight it is
                                  that maketh modest man

❋ "who it is who sits . . ." ❧

who it is who sits
behind the face,
the face of beauty and of truth, both
mere Angels to
that Babe, the howling
Babe

who shall declare
its name, what sits
larger than beauty, than truth
what it is which looks out
on both

can call it God, locked
in its throne of bone,
that mere pea of bone where the axes meet,
cross-roads of the system,
man

discloser, converter, he
will tell, will look out, if you will look,
as long as it takes . . . o E! o Stone!

look, in that face,
and read, an answer, you
who are alone, what we ask,
that we be justly done by,
that what price we pay be more
than beauty or than truth, be
the recognition that we are
of use

one to another separate, but
the form we make by search, by pain
be seen by eyes other
than our own

dedicate, thus, one to another, aid, able
to offer by form justice, the act, the act
crying to be born

to make pride possible, to earn
the knowledge of the Babe, let there by, look!
look! the face is, the face,
in the heart of form the just face is
Love

❀ The Advantage ❀

1

Where do these
   invisible seeds
      settle from?

And how are men able
   to spore them
      into air?

For the gains are
thus communicated.

2

Shall you say
   there are not Powers,
when men spring up on all sides
   (like violets, said Bolyai Farkas)
to a new need)

Men have their proper season, and to that season
   act and image,
      image more than act,
         a rhythm more than image or than act,
proper to them.

3

So if we now again shall call
   the sun a male,
and give him back the moon
   for wife, who'll say
we're wrong? we

who have endured to rotting
   the other way, the making
domestic abstract gods
   of paled-out humans,
father   mother   son

who'll say
   the root of universe
      is not the root of man,

deny
   the edge of mystery is
      the cutting edge,

cry down
   the act of touch, the dumb thing knocking, knocking
at that door?

☀ "Lady Mimosa! deliver us . . ." ☀

Lady Mimosa! deliver us
from all mud

You who took on the job,
keep us at it

Lady, to whom it occurred:
the very brilliance of my flesh
its form
is enough to lead them out;
we follow you

You, who descended,
have the advantage on us:
what you do by fiat
we come up on from fact,
we have
another door

We cherish you,
that you chose to taste
the lazy fruit,
that you got caught:
save us, who are the inverse,
from any indulgence!

You who can breed
with or without aid,
we thank you,
that you made us
as we are.

We understand
this entrance,
comprehend
that entered on

we too uncover ourselves,
are stripped
(as you were)
by their effronteries

        (o Lady, let us also find out
        how to make them blind
        by breast or blow,
        they
        who refuse to know!

        (o Lady, enable us
        to be as able, to be not
confused
        by violence
        (which is also our own)
        to be clear
        that the door we enter by
        we must (as you)
        come up through
        —prisoner!

        let us take on,
        as you,
        the nakedness

        let us know,
        the limits)

You who understood
that the Seven you made stayed too content,
that you had to try to remind them,
to stir them up, we see,
for we have watched us
lulled, even we, your
Limicoli!

See us, as most confronted,
as housed
in the very element we eat on.

Assuage us, then,
when we are as wasps!

You who was curious,
we are

you who stayed tenacious,
we stay

we too will
to take it on!

You,
who by abstraction
made projection,
said form
(with your hip!)
said: difficult,
beauty
is difficult, we

we thank you,
Mimosa!

❋ For Joe ❋

small potatoes, and
gold, golden as she you tumbled
of a black night, as earth
she

small potatoes, and gold
the place yields the dirtied, the dirtiers
and the fine, fine
as her skin

small potatoes
who are ploughed back
and the gold (the black!)
who will live

❋ A Shadow, Two ❦

It is still the cause, the cause, even if the method is

the rods and cones of

a pigeon's eye

        (beauty, sd the Bearded Man

is the inception, is

the continuation, is

in the end

      Enter,

           by the body, its

38 doors!

The 3 Obstacles are

(the Walls which lie flat, which

are of the running, are,

on each of the doors,

lust, ill-will &

stupidity, he sd.

        To fracture facts, by the mind to give back

        (brightness, which the intelletto can, by its play

        reveal documents,

          (I can look on any ass,

          and want it.

          And a little girl.

And not crumple

the flower)

            Sd Gotama:
the emancipation
is to be found in
a habit of mind

       Sd Fleming, wot

is the sound of

thought?)

     We shall have the nouns, the nouns!

     all tied downs

       (Sound, sd Creeley,

I want the

SOUNDS!

❈ De Bono ❈

1

beauty, sd the Bearded Man
is
inception, is
continuation, is
the end   Enter
by the 38 doors!

the 3 obstacles
are (the Walls
which lie flat, which, in fact, are the running)
are,
on each of the doors,
lust, ill-will &
stupidity, he sd

(I can look on any
ass. And want it. And
a little girl.

And not crumple
the flower)

The emancipation,
he argued
is to be found in a habit of
mind

2

Wot, sd Fleming,
is the sound of

thought?

    We shall have nouns, nouns
    all tied
    downs

        Sounds, sd Creeley, I want
        the SOUNDS!

A Day, of a Year

Walkin' 'roun,

goin' along down

walkin' 'roun,

goin' along down

walkin' along

what you had to say about

me

Whistlin',

goin' 'roun,

whistlin',

goin' down,

on the turn

whistlin':

to-each (like as they say)

to-each

his own, to-each

what comes

Walkin' roun

❋ So Gentle ❋

So gentle, nobody seems to have paid him much mind,
as they did Ben

so gentle, when he slipped off to Stratford he left no ripple
    behind,
the Swan

✹ "There are sounds . . ." ✹

There are sounds, but can immoralists

       Two steps up the stairs there was a skirt, a
shining ass swept by a skirt so cunningly I
was all for mounting same right there and then
and then
       And then there was a voice, sat squat on a pillow
over against my own. And the communication
was most direct, most
right along the floor there was, it was, most serious
if the intent is most
serious
       If it is not: I heard, later, that one made one pass
                   at one's wife and
          one kicked one the hell out of one's house

Given such a sound I was given, the voice gave, voice, even
inside. And out, in the storm. In the face of the
      overwhelming shrine
the worship of fear and loss (that peace), to hear such, to
      be presented
it was a rough night, but the soft things, the drive: it is
                        measured out
                          small

We are. But the name of our country is not known, the
      citizens
are hard to find, Boston
or Anacostia.
       Or it is as much there as it is anywhere, for
          where is it
but thee & me, and thee be a bit
as am me, just that little bite, that tittle
of such pleasure, enough: enough
               to make it
               possible

to go forward, the waters up and down, this
     night distinguished
this sound from among those sounds, and the
     lightning
of intent

in the small space, the contracted place
to go on

Question:
     what is it makes us want to, will to, when so
       many . . . When we
     who do not know confusion yet equally we do not
       know clarity, at least
     any other clarity than this, that, suddenly, when
       there is communication
     it matters more than any lust

It is not easy to keep the light in, to keep in what light has
    made its way through, even
this sliding present, this, along this floor in this giddy
    room—o!

     all cleaners and you dirtiers, any
     who cannot hear or refuse to, or even those
     who so much look like new brooms, who may
       be
     better than anything, but
     are they anything in the face of that which
       must which must must be

❋ There are sounds . . . ❋

There are sounds, but can immoralists . . .

                (And then there was a skirt, a
shining ass swept by same so cunningly I
was all for mounting same right there,
and then and then and then

And a voice, sat squat
on a pillow
over against my own pillow
and the communication
was most direct, right along the floor was most
serious
        (if the intent
is serious

If it is not: I heard, later, that one made one pass at one's
        wife, and
        one kicked one the hell out of
        one's
        house . . .

Serious, I was, given, there on the floor, that sound, for
in the face of the overwhelming shrine, overwhelming
worship of, fear, of loss, such quantity
is measured out
so small

We are. But the name of our country is not known, the
        citizens
are hard to find, Boston,
or Anacostia
        Or is it as much there,
as it is anywhere, for where is it
but thee & me, and thee
be a bit, as am me, just that little bite of pleasure, enough
to make discrimination possible texture on out, to go

to go on towards,
                    from among the doubles,
                                        what
we are here for

                    Question: what
makes us want to, who, what is it
saves us from confusion,
                    and its ludicrous consequence, the
                    ukase: DEBUNK
by clarities?

Answer: it is not easy
to keep the light in, to keep in
what light, has made its way through, even
this sliding present, this (along the floor, this, in this giddy
     room o!
          you cleaners, you! who look
          so much like a new broom, who are, yes
          are better than anything but
                              but
but the very thing which must
                    must
that which must
must be!

❋ Signs ❋

fog, and orchid sun
how easily
or cloud, and you can stand to look
at him become a more bright moon
these insubstantial things obscure
his light

as image cause
reality, they
so easily exceed
her (as he), confuse
the even hardened
eye

    (a token, swiped
       from sky: even
       in the city, look, things
       are to be observed, how much
       a man may be misled, then
       headed in, stop
                 THE CAR
    STOP

ah! he!

❋ Glyphs ❋

(for Alvin,
& the Shahns)

I

Like a race, the Negro boy said
And I wasn't sure I heard, what
Race, he said it clear
                              gathering
into his attention the auction
inside, the room
too lit, the seats
theatre soft, his foot
the instant it crossed the threshold
(as his voice) drawing
the whites' eyes off
the silver set New Yorkers
passed along the rows for weight, feel
the weight, leading
Southern summer idling evening folk
to bid up, dollar by dollar, I

beside him in the door

II

I gotta hold of
Hay-foot, Straw-foot

I gotta hold of
a home: yure right!

I gotta hold of
Shiloh

III

Big shots

      throw

            small bullets

❋ "as of what's / ahead . . ." ❋

                              as of what's
ahead
        or what I'd like to see
right now, is
how it is when
the waters are
pink

                for then, surely,
right over our heads, he
would dive like the scarab
he is,   that is, *his*
force is downward, the
     head over heels
     man, the arms
     nor the legs flying
     outwards: not at all
     not at all

Of the Clouds

Out the same picture window the pine bow
Then, it was rain gleaming from the needles, now
it is pale light of morning come and she,

who has just cried (I, too, then, cause
for no tears), with lightness commands me, notice
the quarter moon, how it is there and then it is not there,

how it punctures
its own
sky

✳ The Friend ✸

he was a man made a bank
of the present

> Now if you tally
the present for the future,
and then use it as a past,
there never is any present!

Or that was how it happened,
in this instance, I didn't know it
but I was being racked up,
so many bills, for an account

And, of course, in that present,
I didn't know that was why
I couldn't take it that I had any
value!

What happens, at this end,
when you discover all this?
where are you? who's he?
what about the bank?

It's simple, really — compound
interest and all that. Only

you ain't there, you weren't
there, you was already a

past, you weren't, you couldn't be,
denominations!

So what's he got, for all his capital
operations? Confederate

money. And what can he do with it,
except what Shredded Wheat does?

You weren't there, in the first place,
you was his own small change, and the interest

is all his.

❋ Vinal ❋

Measure by your footsteps, sd the voice.
                                        He
compared his. He sd: counted
is the end of the earth, look, twelve
footsteps. Plus one
where I stand.
                        And the sky and the land leaned
over.
        Thus order
was born.

In the air
there is no death.
                        Man
is thirteen.
                In the cloud-mist
of himself.

Thirteen added, Seven added, One. On the 20th
he raised his voice. Its basis,
asked the sun. And got no answer, the hollows
were still buried, the dawn
had not yet come.

                Anger
came after man. And the ability
to count
                So there were days,
or suns.

This is the count of them.

Black Mt. College—dat ole sphinx— has a Few Words for a Visitor

Name names, Paul Goodman, or we'll have to use your own
the Veryman you make it of the sugar sweet, the ginger
    cookie
Everyman to scare the Witch you, poor boy . . .
                (If you must have us have such classes
as equals, the young, the lads and fearful lasses

                          ((these rimes
Huss too would make, as of so good a man as you here pose
yourself to be, dear you, dear true, dear clear, your poor
dear doom, your going away not rightly used . . .
                    he'd send you
what I send you too, a little reedy Cross sucking food
out of a bottle filled with what now rimes with sis (poor Sis
who don't get half a chance with boys because
her tender ender's such a postern gate it's good
for nothing else than making those young ones you'd lay
    bare—o Paul
who has a rougher thought, who knew he could corrupt an
    army
were it not he had his friends he owed a something to, a rose
perhaps or rose inopportunely on a cop—and there! right on
    the street
or in the middle of Grand Central Palace, look! he showed
what he did not admit he meant

We equals, that is, sons of witches too, cover ourselves with
    cookies
face to face with your fell poem (it fell, all right, four footed
with one foot short where five are called for—five, sd the
    Sphinx
confronted with senescence and with you, still flying from her
and her hot breath who bore you, Hansel Paul, to bore
    us—all

✳ Idle Idyll ✶

          meet me, miss (a white
dais-y

          red rasp-berries
          very damn good, better
          actually

               Until these, I flew
heavily, as the snow heron
flies, or as they call him here, the fish crane
and I prefer that name
                  he
is terrific only
feeding
      (that neck)

           scared
he gallumps like the pelican, lands
by god in trees! about like I do
on a daisy, and I am not
picking berries

            (we look to ourselves
            so perched, like bloated ghosts,
            very damn levi-tate)

            Or has no fight
for the domestic
blackbird, him buzzing
his red spot wings like so,
the wife also in attendance,
and my crane ducks
to get back to the reeds and the position
for fish

The look of things
from a boat on a lake

A Notice,
for All American Mechanics

The luminous physicality of all things,
because each
is an object and an action all at once: the tail, say,
of the beast. Let you
let yr eyes, palms, joints, ears, organs, and skin
have this

Hooked up, and unhookable, is the shingle,
a better way of putting the total,
intelligence — that
you don't have any of the foregoing without
you start churning it on the instant
you get it. Pronto — hondo — the head
goes into the action and takes
what object & motion how far
this known one
can take it

Condition Number Three, the one most, now,
unavailable: character,
the Drummond light, he sd, sheds
light from itself on all sides, the determined
determinant
you are

>   by which, made, you let
>   what light
>   for any other thing, for all things
>   fall

❋ The Picture ❋

live's on it
love's on it
: honor,
on top of the hill
until vertigo
seized him. Fell
into the sea, legs
flying. Was reported
as lost. Last seen
disappearing
into the element
: fear,
of heights. Answered
an ad. Was elected.
And since,
has been charming
newspaper pulp, talks
at the drop of the eye-
wash, shows the white
collar on the crucial
occasion. Is
Caucasian, will not falter
on meeting a lady in a
sarong. Has been known
to cross oceans
on missions
without erring
on arriving, sits comfortably
under awnings where others
would put on all
sail, would even shove
around capes
with the moon stun
up. Is stud
apud
nada, has not sheathe
upon nether, has not parts

for carrying. Carries caps
on foreteeth, hath smile
for beginning, doth call my
to his dog, speaks nicely
into his vision screen, has fat rump
for charcoal, is perishing
by progress, sells selves
on Wednesday, does not cross
Sunday, eats buns
on Monday. Was unanimously selected President
by all odds while wood-lots
stood by themselves and cow birds
laid eggs in other birds'
nests, and the chestnut throated warbler
warbled. Does not make any
misstep.

❋ The Eye ❋

Hopping as they are feeding now it is raining
the sparrows and the two cardinals vex me
as they jerk and interrupt the drabness
outside the window, the grass
and rock and bush and leaves on the slope
one color

❋ The Table ❋

I admit, there are people with whom it is not pleasant
to drink milk, say—and that they should be stayed
the hell away from. Yet, what about those you love,
you say, when, suddenly, they too? So,
in what sense is there anything so small about
to ask a person, please, to pass the milk?
What's—"large"? and for which you argue you'd keep
bitterness?

☀ Ego Scriptor ☀

from love arising
plunge recklessly
forward, the depths
of each manageable,
how to dwell
the sound placed
how love is clear
in the darkness,
Jacopo,
my Jack

cone, of cone departing,
after the slippery sides
who is it arises
free and clear,
out up the light, is he worth
a song, Jack?

It pierces, I am tossed
side to side, how
to tell all, how say it is
to plunge straight, going
where you know — how sing,
Jacopo, two eyes
that slay me
suddenly

❋ For P V himself alone and god bless him ❋

He sd he wore it
like clothes, that it was not
his skin

As it was decidedly not as another, had it
the other way, that it was so cool inside
at his Aunt's, the clay vats
swelled
(as Voulkos's do,
and came to such fine feet,
he used to get inside
by the ladder,
and take his siesta
                    (the thought pressing,
of the wine
poured over him

And I, again,
with the world on me.
And she sd, "I reflect
it, am riding,
if briefly,
in a Packard)
                    the way it is,
outside: briefly,
quickly
that inside,
it does,
swell,
no matter
            that the coolness
of a vat
is not
transatlantic
            (even if it is also not hollow,
that hollow-

mobile of,
the transmontane)

One loves both,
the inside and
what he also does: he colors
from itself/ by fire/ into
as stones are
                (not clay
as melon, as
caves are, for honey,
or bears, neither
concrete or
the venturesome
                (what she sd,
"It ain't nothing
but money, that's what's so nice about
what I have on,
at this moment"

As that life is which
is not to be slept in,
we cry who
love those clothes more
than we love sleep or
beauty, who wear
the swelling thing as
he throws 'em, inside

—and out: to do it, not
to make it anything more,
neither to lend it, or
to borrow

nor to be pretty about
what is shrewd

The world
is cool

two eyes, a nose

It is round,

very good looking clothes.

And,
a race

✳ The Feast ✴

I

sacred sycamore and the odor
of cedar wood (the odor
of the buried boat,

trying to keep up with
the day (the sun going

as fast as it does go.

At least three-decks. Linen
gear. And celestial
stuffs. How to voyage

through the night (the same kind of
measures of
the irretrievable

passing (even though they do
— the measurers —
repeat themselves.

88 pieces of limestone
for a sky, over

— which we walk on, wearing
neither the day nor the night, neither
the past nor the
palpable.

Slung

between stone,

and wood

II

Rather,

the red bird buffing
two lead figurines to give to
another

figure.

Or the tiller
gone in the mouth of
a crocodile.

The other
condition.

Actually,

the waters: not anything

buried in

anything, least of all
things: not in the night

not the sand

not the fishes'
mouths

                    Solely,

              the Diorite

            growing up through

            the sea,

                          the towering
                          figure

III

In fact crumbles,
that sort of
past: to be sealed
for after
the feast-day

Or to be looked over
by those who have the nose for
baked meats

Either.

As it is it is not
pictures (which smell
likewise—that is,
of Lebanon, before or after
Ramadan

            (who giggles
at him squat
before the idol.

The game is quicker
than nature

than water. Much quicker

than the snapping
jaws

       than the day (the night

       very fast.

For the Children, in the Novel, Mr. Hellman

Sunday, Monday, Tuesday, Wednesday,
all the girls have got the frenzy
Thursday, Friday, Saturday, Sunday
all the week the boys are randy

✳ The Retort ✳

The notochord
is enough

Plus gills,
that is, that

the thing wants to
breathe

as well as
stand up

Bound so,
there is

society
enough:

the chordates
replace

the Eighteenth
Century

Mind you, if
the breathing

apparatus is
admitted

to have to be
elementary:

the nose
is Pittsburgh

Otherwise,
you have Becket

Massachusetts,
or Woodstock

New York: the root
not yet

cut off from, the cry
still mew

the howl
of the survivor

not heard, only the radical
new

not the old newly
emitting, the

conch blasting
the semidome,

the interference
shouldered off

all that falls
of its own weight

let fall, and I
clearing only

straight through to
the sky, being

the tentpost, you
and I, clearing

standing on arsis
to rise, making

that one thing,
concurrence,

concussive

❋ "This is Thoth speaking" ❋

a man is a name of a nome
when a man is a nome his name
is a man

❋ So Help Me ❋

yes mam, I'm a
mam of words,
mam

❊ The Old Physics Restored, or, Newton on Man ❊

(a recently discovered manuscript of a poem)

Man's day, he both knows and knows the day,
except for the sun, has no regularity. Or has,
on a scale which makes his day a death, and thus
the same as what a day is, a mere unit of seasons,
nature's pushing, so many trees to fill out rings
or bees to fill out bees or hives, or beasts
for market, crops for beasts. Or men. The wind
has no order, nor snow, rain is only, and soil,
an intention, the day, on a path man
cannot complete. He can only watch the sun
do what no man can, declare the day.
But in that declaration declare
man's day as well.

                    Night! night, precision
he can read as he himself is overhung
by orders, included in darkness where movement
—and not the moon's, the moon's
the season of the night as the sun is
the order of the day—Orion
stares at man glaring in his action, Charles' Wain
goes upside down in hours, decants
and yet the next night is back in like position to attempt
    again
to break the tether or the tropism holds him
to the Fixed Star, man's skies are permanently twisting
fixed and unfixed patterns and recurrences trysting
passing on in changes yet each night returning
to try again an ordered motion to make the self he can
    complete
as the tree he also is completes itself but differently. He
    can,
only by the night of his being in which order lies

History is what his day is. Urania is the other study
from which the seven sorts of song come. Man can make
        his species
total season and see in season sense his own death balks
        him at
but the stars, her governance, nightly repeated as daily
the Big Star does what those do who live in the darkness—
        nightly
man sees sets and upsets, losses, Venus gone for weeks
but she returns in symmetry-asymmetry to fix him as he
        did not know .
the North Star does not budge, and anyhow, his poles
are as her rotations not as the firm one only valuable to
        ships.
The whole sky, at night, is man's book in which he sees
        himself,
with Moon to bind him to his day.

                O Memory who is the mother,
and forgetfulness the forgotten father, let man retake the
        night.
The day has dispersed him, and the night he throws up
        cities
to prevent him from, while both go on as he does, double,
        as he is
and hold out to him the two he is, as he has two to do,
to order and intend. O History, o Urania, o

seven songs!

❋ O'Ryan—#11 ❋

1

say   day   a per-son
can be
known a mythologem

man,
by nature, you can say no more than

brown
cow, you can say no more than

moo-th
ōs

say   day
long men munch
hassle   rassle, you can say no more than
Fasten

2

fire fire
be can no more can be
earth air,
is not water, is familiar

If he's estranged

be can no more can be, he's
lazy
      Or is unwilling.
If he's mad,
you'll know it

3

Tell a
animal
tale
      (Angel?
      de-
mon?
      Prog-
nosis.)
      Froggie, the children
play
      lay each other, pre-
tend.
      And then they say, for real.
Will you—or you?
You better you
frog you

4

Who speaks against man speaks
himself

hair
of the dog he is. Who has words

more than who he is, lies. Myths

are not that. Thoughts

are as acts or we are all

metaphysicians. Beasts

and metaphysicians.

     The child says,

don't look at me!

5

     It is not how things are,
it is how we say they are.

     How do we say it?

Say: once a man was walking down, and he put a
     bone, and

ketchup!

     Or polka-dottie and a policeman

Do you leave it, will you play, with my toys? Do you?

It's another form

of dog

     bone of his mother

✳ Thoughts of the Time ✴

The fields of the sky.

A hot moon low in the west.

In it, as in a net a spring blade
might sit, not gleaming

As in a pocket, not saying anything.

In it

✳ Add an Edda ✴

Flat are the waters. Soferforth
have things gone. Soggarth
is useless, and godhead

is down. That which fills up
is mixed up. The animate
is sunk in it, cute

is the natural. Dampa-stead
no good and Micklegarth
we don't go to. New Rome

is Mindinao

Sub-title:
OR SINK ME SWEET

❋ How One Feels About It When It Goes Good ❋

swing out sweet bells

of verse   /

        /

     not your tongues

but what is struck

is tune

❋ Anniversary ❋

on the north side of the telephone pole wet snow stuck
the nation
is all right,
Walt

fire-engine-red truck alongside less-interesting red of
        De Soto convertible, Walt
they're still making things, WW
and have a Dept
of Commerce

a boy paints watery pink from 5 & 10 Cent Store palette,
and the sweat in his hair from the heat of the oil stove
predicts
he could grow up to be a very attractive street car
        conductor,
if they had street cars
which they don't

No one would say that Ontario's shore is blue, that is,
one doesn't care as much for color as such as,
or taste, or owning anything, even not, even staring
into photographers' windows on F Street, bracing
the storms
of the nation

Walt, you look too good. You front. We don't. We
—you know, you're
bracing? It's either a Civil War of Abraham Lincoln's
the size: "big,"
sez the boy, for everything, he wants the
most

Believe me, Walt
they do

Only, you wouldn't
sense it

from the color
of the toilet

or the tissue

Or the menstrual

blood

❋ "future / open . . ." ❋

             future

open the beyond
underworld exits and entrances
the smoke going up among the stars

shivering ware
in Athens the dust

      and elsewhere a pine and
      oak

            dusty olives

      in the sea green

                Wind

is a strong man

   ichor is blood

                      what dies
    on the ground   must be born,
                      they said

            to drink
            memory after

               forgetfulness

     raise up the dead he's a
     machine

       walking so stiffly

         both

sleeping and awake

in its junction the soul
had memory to go by

❋ And Now: The World! ❦

"Enemies"? Define,
pliz. In the visione,
China über alles

Russia? second-rate
America? flukes,
from Ten Thousand Ugly

leadership. When invaders
come in, men burrow themselves
in time while mule teams

BULLSHIT sd the
poet MAHn sd he
one endless priceless

fresco. Über alles is
PUGAR Campeachy "RE-
FRESCOS" (the hilltown,

"Lerma," the conductor
lazieth (as in the picture
distance — through which passes

us, our priceless noses burning up
from the air. You're ON,

MON!

How It Was Joseph Altschuler ✷ Brought Us Up To Be

Covered with
feathers. Or to be altogether archaic, one Hercassian boar's
pelt, as, previously you had done in one lion and slung
his skin over your shoulder.

A bow, always
a bow. The
weapon

Now the story. White. Paint the face white
white paint all white on the outside
A clean shirt front

On which wear one
string
tie

and not break
a twig. Break
their necks.

❋ Assuming the Soul Is a Bitch ❋

That, then, becomes one Have
no fear
        Doubt not except
the doubt which troubleth all

Ok a Brooklyn gun Place the shot
on the moon Diatomic power, Lady

of my insides Crash program
Mr Big who fucks

all the time Or wants
to

        Neither
vegetable nor natural neither

gender Neither all
the gab

        Neither
ma nor pa

        nor
Willy-grand Upside

        Nor
downtown—naw, sd the girl

writhing
on the white iron bed, from the white salesman trying
to force her

        Neither
sex nor mind

        Nothing

A Greeting To
❋ A Lord High Canadian ❦
Lawyer's Wife

I'd wash her ass
with shamanism

lift up her skirts
and dose her good

for bed or table
she's not able

the way she goes off
at the mouth

Eve,
and Lilith
and Adam
and Pie

Couples couples
in the bars
in stores
on the streets
in restaurants
—on the grass

Families
gone down
to two
—in the cities

Volume
—and credit
shrink
the unit:
quality control

Merchandise
man
and woman

❋ "a rivulet of soil . . ." ❋

a rivulet of soil   a horny
   rock
      a house
with a fish tail
and feet

        a yellow house
by a green stream
a woman
     at the door
says her father
       is at work
right now

    Magno-Lithic
    Verse

✳ The Gleeman Who Flattered You ✿

as tomorrow as soon as it is day
you shall go out and lose your
friends and family and they
shall curse you lightly, bare you'll
go and leave the world's glory
now poor seasons and the castle gone
back to gulls the poor palace
of all the life, with worms now
shall be your stopping place
the place you sleep is built so cold
you'll whimper like the voices of
sailors scratching hulls fathoms down
the whole ocean a roof to rest upon your chin

✳ Thy Gleeman who Flattered Thee ✿

as tomorrow as soon as it is day
you shall go out and lose your
friends and loves and they shall
give you a once over lightly, bare
you'll go and have to leave the
world's altogether, now made poor
seasons and your castle   gone back to
the gulls, the poor palace
of life   with worms now shall be
your stopping place and sleep
is built so coldly you'll scratch like those drowned sailors
mewing outside the telephonic hull
to get in, fathoms down hundreds of
miles out, the whole ocean a roof
resting on your chin

✽ The Intended Angle of Vision ✽

Hammond's Castle
da allure of German
expressionism, the pond
of Western Harbor and

Stage Head a fair
Tsukiyama sansui, the water
silver and ochre where
it was, a previous time

black and gold, when I rowed it
as a young man. Right now a boat
peels off the ochre
and runs silver over

❋ The Yellow Mask ❦

Only a few faint elements of order hint
in the yellow of the mask

Not shapes, dimensions or measurability
in the yellow of the mask

God has not travelled
in the yellow of the mask

In the yellow of the mask
the light has just been lit

❋ "A direct downward path . . ." ❦

A direct downward path
in the yellow of the mask

Out the back
in the yellow of the mask

From yourself
in the yellow of the mask

The circumambience
in the yellow of the mask

❋ The Hustings ❋

*A Poem Written to Leroi Jones Two Days After
the Election of John Fitzgerald Kennedy to
the Presidency of the United States*

the future sucks
all forward,
now   The past

has been removed
by progress   Cuba
wants to make its own

sugar   The Soviet Union
has already
contaminated

the Moon   China
wants to destroy
the United States

Leroi Jones
spits out
the Nation

I do,
too   I stay
at home

I do not
go abroad   I like
the west end

of Main Street
the policeman
of the beat

I greet
crossing the street
off duty

in his topcoat
        Ben Smith
the new President's

roommate
Joe at Tally's
making fun

of what boots
it would take
to clothe me

if I wear overshoes
on a damp day
like today   The girl

in the
Waiting Station
says the colors

of the scarf
and the green hat I wear
clash

I took em off
so, I said, she
can see me

I try to kiss
my wife
as she gets on

the bus   She says not
on the street
I go off

feeling like
the President
receiving the plaudits

of the populace
on a day
when Leroi Jones

has asked me
it seems to me
to say why

one should continue to live
in the United States
when newspapers

tell lies
about everything
which goes

on And the new president
says
longrange

American
views   Underneath
the eyes

of the human
race I cry lies
on a future now

is the pasty-face
of young girls and boys
lift the cock

in my pants
to my woman's behind
The open-ended

character of future
says to me Leroi
Jones stay

in the age
of your nation
when

all those new
nations want
is the lies

your own nation
gives
to the sun,

that the sun
is a fire germs
of the race

can't give back for the life
we are walking
the streets on fire

with ourselves
for wares
for exchange

for the fire
of our cocks
in the ass

of the woman
we love

and without any
abaissement
to the new child

of the new
President   France also
has been deprived

of the past and the youth
of the world is already in love
with wrist-watches

I am in love with
you   Are you in love
with the future?

Do you believe
in what has been your life?
Or in these bundles

of the promise
of the use
of human beings

en masse? democracy
en masse en
transistors? I don't believe

in planets any more than
I believe than one thing more
that any one of us is short

is good enough

to answer
the question: how life equals
its own

creation   In the eyes
of men and women
is the race

they run, and election
is their own, demanding
that they have everything

an uncontaminated earth
shall offer them. And afterwards
their

sophistication
not in the rumpus
and the crowds

of present
popular
sovereignty. It isn't the moon

which is in danger
but that the singleness
of the sun

which is neither soviet
nor capitalist
made be made into a cheap

One   Leroi Jones
my name is Charles Olson
I live at 28 Fort Square

Gloucester Massachusetts
in the world. Otherwise
I am what I am able

to do. I believe,
I would like to die
with my eyes

as open
as I imagine
the only way one can imagine God's eyes is

they are open
forever
in contemplation

of any one of us, that creation
can only close
when those eyes

and our own
can look into
the same fire

that we don't have anything
no matter what a future
except not to be blinded

in that we have to also
stare into

what is as hidden
as it is to His
eyes because

we are whatever
the human race
can be in the imagination

required of it that it be
what it was imagined to be
that it has existed

and that it exists
at all.
If necessity exists

and you and I are as much examples as crowds demanding
youth taking and the new inventing
ways to have more,

there is no let-up
and no giving over
to crowds youth or

invention,
and this string
which ties me to you

and to John Cronin policeman
in topcoat
at this end

two days after
the election of a man I happen
to know

as president
of the United States,

no matter that its fate
is second-rate, now
and that the New Frontier

is decadence and the future
is the race's future
all over the place   No one can

as Gerrit Lansing said
commemorate energy   Our life
Leroi Jones

is not an energy
like the sun's   Our life is a purpose
of a string or thread forced out of

our own eyes as the string of a spider craving
to meet the eyes of the purpose
of what we call the eyes

of the fire in the eyes of the blood of
our own creation; that one's mother and father
put one

on the earth is the sun's
doing and the rest of it
is what one means by why

one is alive. I don't think there is anywhere
but where I am
which can bring me closer

to what I shall look like
when if I do look
as I would look

out of my eyes
into John Cronin's
or yours

or John Fitzgerald Kennedy's
whose eyes?
when? where

that matter
of the future
is more yours

and mind than at this moment the deliverable
is patently probable
the world over? Good enough

that all shall eat
and have the television view
of the waters

which surround
and have made brightest Venus
of all stars except the sun and the moon

for all the years so far
of the human race   I don't care
that water

is the atmosphere
of Venus or that pop
is the drink

of the masses   I care
that there is not enough known yet to support you
in your eyes

or myself
in mine. When that day comes
that the moments that I do believe

are strung strong enough like what looks like spit
which a spider makes those strings of
I'll have the ability to wire you

Please come immediately
There is no need to worry
All is here

❋ Trivittata ❋

whelks
gourmandizing
on like pink flesh
—gelīc—and turning hard
matter out of your way

eating through sea city slums
like the police and seeing results,
pimpled whelk,
I'm sick of your worm-holed victims
on the shore

attracted in mobs
to dead things
you are all over

❋ Where They Came From ❋

young persons came in today
from the rain jungle, their glee
almost was that you could not imagine
rain or sogginess so dark
men could cut off other men's heads
with one blow of a stiff sharp knife
wielded like a ceremonial sword
and that these youngers
had fled because life
was impossible in such a
dusk place, surprise
was so easy they left
& one of them is eating corn
and beans out of two plates
at the table with myself
eating one

❋ The Osiris Boat ❋

with Santy Claus at rest on its
deck stretched out full length
in the Cappadocian moonlight

or Saint Andrew full spread eagle
in his Cross Anatolian
coolness: how many

Milesians do you know,
Phrygians, some even part
Thracian? have you no feeling

for the color of the cloth of the
rug hung for a sail to get you
off the nut? I am *not*

Danubian Illyrian or
Tyrrhenian sd the dismembered Corpse
when he was altogether again

& sat up straight

❈ The Snow 2 ❈

falling in water there is no end
to snow down as up
there is no end to the falling in love
of men and women
     the snow falls in the water so

❈ *Kar-cha-ro-donta* ❈

cast them into the heaving sea from the continent,
so kept drifting long time up and down the deep,
and all around kept rising a white foam from
the immortal flesh

     (and in it a maiden was nourished

❋ Apoptic ❦

for Richard Bridgeman

re-entry, without pillow, dear and the pieces
all melted to drops some passing as carriers,
motors from the airport into Springfield, hubby
darling otors for fences to drain off
the glue —
              the life-giving fluids re-enter
the evident, cell we dance?

off high in heaven observing the uselessness,
the cracks in Charles' Dish he said to the Lady, "Muse,
the ditch you shall always have with you but me?" as he
      terere
came down through the transmission wall

Bursts in the teeth the old Cosian drops
bought a net and drew up in it aw gee pa when
do we turn around? in this huge building isn't there
a place to pee? Signed off then when the cushion at his
      back
flew into so many pieces of violent river-bottom

✹ "all covered with feathers . . ." ✹

1

all covered with feathers
is the baby bird
born of the morn
before the dawn

out from the egg
or happy in
the shell
swam in the waters

worked himself over
from where he wasn't
wanted himself to be

passed into the hole
in the egg's wall
to satisfy his
desire

walked the path
of the two men
whom he'd heard
had left

the tribe as they promised
and were said
to have disappeared
in a cave

in the well's wall

2

where the toc holds on
to the white chalk

and talks
as he plays
from the top

to a branch, flying
a green color
        as sharp

as color
can be
when he darts
to the nest,

if it is,
or branch
which is half-way
from the surface

to the well's rim

3

or his call
is as dry
in the open
enclosed
place

the toc bird's
toc
as the sound

of the being
of Paul
Fat today

whom I love

and who shined
my shoes in his parlor
so small
with my knees

and his
size
I had to shift
my left foot

to the right iron rest
so he could
get himself
in position

to use the tight cloth
to give my shoes
the last
lustre a shoe

requires

❋ Is Black ❋

the Mother the Negro and the Englishman
the independence has recreated itself
we walk away black in the encounter
the world is full of light

the rich magnolia blossoms in a week
she can go to the temple for herself
did anyone except one ever make
a full confession I can't do
except what you have told me I shall
Expectancy has fallen
on the briar

The Mother is a monster because nature
once was prime. We shall give love
as we pass by. Commodity

has dwindled to itself. Inherence

is black

❋ In an Automotive Store ❋

in an automotive store
which is like a stock room anyway
a homely City girl and I

flirted, that is I skated
around in front of her
as she stood

on the other side of a counter
from me.

A messenger came in with a piece of rubber
& some small metal part attached to it
which was from my car

and he told me that the police
wanted me to come and identify
or take the car away

But I suddenly realized
the car was in Connecticut
and not here in the City at all

As I went out
the entrance
was a hall

like in a rotunda
and a salesman
was putting out new

auto electrical inventions
like at a Fair, a table of batteries & cable poles like strips
and my son

had grabbed hold,
and wouldn't let go

of these connections

and I had to tear him
off by sheer ugly strength
and I was embarrassed

before the salesman, ogling him
at the child I had, as I lifted my son off

directly & stiffly
up & down & bore him
out the door

❋ "The nation / is nothing but poetry . . ." ❦

for Ann Denahy
in retaliation

The nation
is nothing but poetry
The universities
are sties
John Wieners
has suffered enough
Catholics
are ashamed of the body
The soul
inhabits the body   Main Street High Street connected by
College where my auto
jumped over
the crosswalk   The sign read
your body
is to drop
its load
      your body
is a holy
thing
    your body
is a wave
of Ocean
      your eyelids
will reveal your soul, your mouth will your clothes
will fall off from you
when you do

❋ The Grain of December ❋

the ordered
coming and going
of December

the rising,
and setting of,
December

the waxing
and waning
of December

has raised
my hackles
and riz

my umpus
and led me
to the point where December

must go
from the calendar
as men have exorcized before

whatever
wrongs them
because it does

set against
their
grain

152

✴ "I met my Angel last night . . ." ✴

I met my Angel last night or it was the corner
of Reservoir Road. He was me allright or it was I
went right ahead doing what I had intended, inviting
him to go with me on a train ride from that corner
to see a grand scenery I had been told or knew was
supposed to lie along the bank of a river which wld
be on the right as one rode the train down into the
City—was a fully developed subway or surface train
even Reservoir Road was a complex of the City, and had
never myself taken this trip, so off we went even though
I thought he was blind and henceforth the scene was his,
inside the train. He got a passenger sitting beside me,
on my left, to shoot craps with him—in the aisle, was
his point, and he made very evident he thought that was
what you did if you shot craps you played where you were
and looked over his shoulder at any conductor might be in
the car behind as though to point out to either the fellow
beside me or myself that one did this whether or not there
were any objection. I observed then, as he stood there, that
he was not a bum, as I had also thought, or that there was
anything shabby about him, if there were he was in control
and commanding as much of his being as one might, holding
himself in his shape and ability, and, on the point at hand,
shooting craps, that he was able. It was this, his ability,
which showed itself when we were back again at the corner
the original corner where the restaurants were (we never
did get to the scenery). He was by this time some sort of
a counterman or short order cook himself, at least he was
standing behind a counter at which I and, on my left again,
two eaters, one of whom (the one nearest me) was an old
friend who has long been a loaded finger-pointing pal of
mine. The two of them were finishing up a cheesecake pie
while I and my shadow looked on, and the three of them
were on the side of how good the food was in a restaurant
at the same corner, to which I disagreed. The climactic
point came when my old friend clinched the argument by
claiming how good the cooking was there, even to the fried

partridge or pheasant day penises! At which point the
    Angel
turned to me and demanded I give back to him a fish I
    didn't
even know I was carrying. Which I passed over the counter
    to him,
and that was that.
                        The final scene took place shortly
    thereafter
when (still thinking he was blind) I tried to sneak, for my
    son,
a clipping or coupon off what later turned out possibly to
    be the
same fish but at that moment was some generalized object
    of which
this coupon was a part. Then it was my Angel clearly
    revealed he
saw everything which was going on and with equal dignity
demanded I put the coupon back, with severity
    pointing out to me that
our name—his or mine or my son's or his mother's also—
    was
written on the coupon and like a stock or bond piece was
    there-
fore only valuable in place. And so despite its perforated
    edges
for removal, that I put it back where it belonged. Which I
    also
sheepishly did.

✻ "There is a goddess / of earth . . ."

There is a goddess
of earth and heaven and sea
The earth, or Hell, is wealth,
which she gives, in two forms
& each person requires. The confusion,
here, is mother — food, and self-
esteem, behind which hides money,
which all men, and women, do get,
willy-nilly. Her influence, as mother,
contaminates sex. Sex and society
are therefore her true aspect,
and when she is presented
in her true aspect, her power
as earth is plenty — the City
is filled with persons, it is itself
filling, she is as rich as her counterpart,
Pluto, who is the King of Plenty
as well as the King of Hell
— and absconds with daughters
(Eubolos was taking care of his
sheep in the field when
suddenly the earth opened
into a hole in itself
and down went the sheep
as into a chute at the same time
he heard horses' hooves and a chariot
came sweeping up with a driver
whose face was hidden but Eubolos
could see him strangling a girl
beside him with one hand
while he drove the horses
straight into the earth)
and the one, when the daughter
has been rushed off with,
whom the mother, when she hears
from Eumolphus what Eubolos
did see, and knows for sure

this was her daughter and it is Hell
who has stolen her, the mother
has to turn herself to the goddess
to get Zeus to get Pluto to admit
he has the girl—and to trade
for her future. The goddess
is the goddess of transaction
she is not life and death,
Nature is life and death,
the goddess is the protectress
of the true Night, the Night
which never ends, the Night
which turns its face as the Day
does, Night which shifts,
no one ever doesn't want more
Day. Black Night, which frightens
the soul, black Night whose god
is Hell (whom light always
relieves, whom the motor Day
chases so easily around
to the next Night, whom Dawn
demolishes by simply suffusing
with the light of her lover,
each man is a son each woman is
a daughter at the beginning
of each Day   and Dawn
is a secret of that light) but Night
is a light of man and woman, Night is driven
back on itself, Night itself is slept in,
Nature is, and Hell alone
shakes night, only Hell, only the God
of Hell breaks in on such
slumbers, and awakens
the living ones. Then Wealth
falls as Zeus came down
on Danae as Kore came back
through the split in the earth
—and the goddess of earth

Zeus favors her,
of all goddesses
and thus gives her the power
to grant wealth—which his brother,
who is only Black Zeus, who is only
the sun on the other side, who is only
Night—she is only Night, Night is only
richness, and hell, the blackness
is only the precarious
12 hours of darkness (which, like the Year
is only in balance twice in the year
at the equinoces, all the rest of the time
is danger the day is greater the day
is shorter Night is eating
the Day the Day has intruded
on the Night until in December,
all is in Danger, God himself
may go down to Hell

Life is not in danger
where the goddess
is concerned—any more than Pluto
endangers. He takes only
the Earth's own Daughter
down, to refine her, after
too many years with the Mother,
to teach her that Plenty
doesn't come only from Nature
by Nature, that as she is a woman
of her own self she participates
in the light, she has order
she has work to do, her mother
isn't the only one who has work
to do, the father teaches the daughter
she also is a woman, her mother
is only his woman, only a god
can teach a daughter how extricated
she is from the gifts, of Nature
on her own she will think it all comes

from herself, that all she has to do
is emulate her mother, the God of Hell teaches
she is herself a principle—and the goddess
here spoken of is the one who guarantees
each daughter will keep her marriage
to the God of Hell, that part
of each year she'll spend
part of each instant of the light
of the day and of the night
she'll spend as his wife,
her own Black Father. Pluto
is the God of the Black Sun,
Pluto is the God of Night
—and the goddess, as the power
of plenty, is black,
she is the blackness
of the roots and of water
and of the cracks in rocks
She is the goddess
of heaven—as Zeus
here too prefers her
to his daughter of the
mountains and his son
the god of the sun
who are each representatives
of the way but not
of the meaning: she is
a figure of meaning
Zeus even made her
a special function:
she is one [of] those who
see dawn
with their own eyes
—dawn which is itself
far-seeing or sees
any thing—the moment
of awakening shoots up
the matter and the attention
from the earth to heaven—

anyone who has acquired
a reason to think of
daylight as an instance
and a condition, as not
solely conditional or
accidental — they
may remind themselves
of her and notice
that she stands in the
midst of the meeting
of Night and Day
and not as the goddess
of cross-ways not
the shooter she,
this cousin this niece
is the Queen of Light
the Half-Wife of God
the one who doesn't [know] or care
for what the Wife
knows — the knowledge
of the world's fate,
that her husband
created it and then can imagine
its end — this "daughter-
wife" born of a mother
whose husband may not
have been the cause of
the girl's birth, is placed
by Zeus to act for men
and women as though she were
almost he, all except
that one same thing Hera
knows, otherwise
the goddess
knows and contributes
exactly because she doesn't
have to do with the end of the world
the animus of man and woman
offers them the belief

that the Light
is before Heaven and Earth
that as they wake in the morning
they wake before Morning woke
that Day is later than
they are that the quarters
of the hours the three quarters
of the day itself that Night,
when it comes, is later than
they, this is the goddess
of heaven, this is the goddess
on the other side of the light;
if Night requires her Light
requires her
as the nurse of youth
(as the nurse of a man
and the nurse of a woman)
as the Light of the Night
is known.

She is the goddess
of heaven, she is the goddess
of the sea

❋ "the wild geranium . . ." ❋

the wild geranium
who looked at me
and my own face
was of the same size as it

❋ "Planted the fruit skin & all . . ." ❋

Planted the fruit skin & all 2″
into the soil, tended same 8 years and
only one plant was worth the saving

Wales Bull his name was, had favored
horticulture to his trade, which was
gold-mending, and was not a nursery-man

Previous to him there had not been the Concord
grape, there had been the Catawba
and the one he crossed with it, the Isabella

He planted the fruit skin and all
2″ into the ground, and covered the row for those years
with wooden planks, to get the one plant which

Was worth the saving Planted the fruit skin & all
was worth the saving

❋ "Oh! fa-doo: the enormous success of clerks . . ." ❦

Oh! fa-doo: the enormous success of clerks
due to the even greater success of Agency men

Oh! for a man because myself have seen his demeanor
no less civil than he excellent in the quality he professes!

besides divers of worship (Gentlemen) have reported
his uprightness of dealing, which argues his honesty,

— and his facetious grace in writing that approves his art"

Oh! the Beauty who had his Heart wrapped in a Woman's
Hide!

❋ "You need never fear . . ." ❦

You need never fear you never
go away from the center
                    Your soul
continues to do its
business   You are monitored
from it   you are instructed
        And now the Mother & Daughter
are unionized   You have stolen
the cuckoo tipped
Sceptre

❋ "Jim Bridger first white man . . ." ❦

Jim Bridger first white man into Yellowstone
thought God had flipped if this was Creation

❋ Have Them Naked Instead ❦

wageearner versus
woman, who prostrates
herself she spreads her legs
for a man
to come into her and she can wait
until he does or after he has
until he does again or issues
from her
children — a man
fucks differently And can get fucked
right here he gets
no issue in the same sense she
does she cannot lose
if she lets down
her milk she is beautiful
right where she all
goes on he goes
elsewhere

      LET IT BE SAID, SAID THE SLEEPER
WHO WAKED UP AFTER FIFTY YEARS
IN THE LABYRINTH, DELIBERATELY
LOSING

      Said Epimenides

- 2
    (Saturday June 6 LXIV

❋ "Barbara Whirlwind . . ." ❦

Barbara Whirlwind
Italian Sandwich

❋ My Goddess ❦

Saw me into the other worlds, gave me the push which
    opened
their doors. Also could have ridden me
to death, such beautiful fucking she was given to,
capable of, had made herself able in, my Mare

upon whose back—or she upon my belly—
or on my left side tossing up her interfering nightdress
or clothes I rode
into the worlds

> (the Tree of Life blooms
> in the Cunt, the Tree of Life grows
> in the Cunt, in the Cunt is the
> Universe in which the Tree of Life
> stands

❋ Lovers ❋

She is frank he is
tender He is
Woman She is
Man My

Cocking, more
Music in the New Found Land. Father
come ashore, Mother
stretched to
more: Lover,

                    (10,000
brillionth sons racing
12
of the 15 billionth
years

of My Land My Lover Ever
More: poly
anthro-
both come to, home to
me,

My Father, My First Beloved, My Lovers —

more

❋ "These people and their / Amusement Park . . ." ❦

These people and their
Amusement Park.

Like horses, bored, and finding
anything (which comes to the fence, or
offers itself) di-
verting. Turns them on.

While the Earth
groans

❋ "Melville's sense of blooming late. . . ." ❦

Melville's sense of blooming late.
The "Century" Plant.
From staying up all night as
Urania, for example. And "warning" all Virgins
"everywhere." "Armed," etc. As though he could hide his
    own love affair ´
or condition.
Like Whitman, by reversing the gender.
Or carrying the thing off somewhere else,
                     and making it drastic. Or
                          romantic.
And we wouldn't know.

❋ February, 1968 ❋

traverse
& —— "Transit" of

                  sort out
                  in the midst of
                  and because of
                  futuristics

question whether
anyone other than
Giap & for that purpose

        otherwise all is
        Muslim and
        we move baldly to
        the situation *before* the
        laying down of Heaven & Earth.

EDITOR'S NOTES

❧ **EDITOR'S NOTES** ❧

THE FOLLOWING notes provide a date of writing for each poem, a brief publishing history (for those previously published), a description and location of the manuscript used for this edition, followed by other information that might be useful for reading the poems, including the identification of the more obscure references and allusions. Abbreviations used are: *CP* for *The Collected Poems of Charles Olson,* ed. George F. Butterick (Berkeley: University of California Press, 1983); *HU* for *Human Universe and Other Essays*, ed. Donald Allen (New York: Grove Press, 1967); *Maximus* for *The Maximus Poems,* ed. Butterick (Berkeley: University of California Press, 1983); *O/C* for *Charles Olson & Robert Creeley: The Complete Correspondence,* ed. Butterick, vols. 1–8 (Santa Barbara; Santa Rosa: Black Sparrow Press, 1980–1987); and CtU for Literary Archives, Babbidge Library, University of Connecticut, Storrs.

Birth's Obituary ❧

Written 1941. Previously unpublished. An alternative version of "You, Hart Crane" (*CP*, 4). This is the original version under this title; a revised version in *CP*, 4. Undated TS on unwatermarked paper at CtU, found in folder "1949-8 — & back" along with other poems from ca. 1941 to 1949; folded as if for mailing and revised in pencil. Dated "1941" in sheet of notes from February 1945. See also Olson's letter to Creeley, 23 June 1950 (*O/C*, I, 145): "Did do, come to think of it, a verse on hart [Crane]! the 1st days i ever did same . . ." He goes on to indicate the poem was written while living in New York on Christopher Street, i.e. ca. October 1940–April 1941, and continues: "I called hart, new archeopteryx. And do have that feeling, that he was, somehow, some marvelous throw-back, a vestigia, forward, in that sense, surely. . . . Yes. I had it, this way: You who made a bridge / leaped."

Orizaba (l. 6) was the ship from whose deck Crane leaped to his death in 1932; named after the Mexican city and volcano. "As another did in chains" (l. 11) refers to Christopher Columbus, on the return from his third voyage to the New World (1498–1500). Crockett (l. 13) is the American frontier hero, Davy Crockett (1786–1836).

"Atalanta ran swift course . . ."   ❀

Written 1941. Previously unpublished. An alternative version of "Atalanta" (*CP*, 5). Undated TS on unwatermarked paper at CtU, heavily revised. Original title, "Atalanta," crossed out, as is an original 1. 12 — "I, Orpheus, sing." — and a final stanza: "A faun you gave / Metempsychosis into human: / — Memory loins shall lave / Till we are shade, o woman!"

Along with "Mavrodaphne," or its alternative "White Horse" (*CP*, 6), one of Olson's earliest poems — according to the poet in conversation, 1968 — written after first meeting his wife, Constance Wilcock, in May 1940. A poem titled "Atalanta" dated "1941" on sheet of notes from February 1945. Another undated, unrevised TS sent the Guggenheim Foundation with a version of "White Horse" before 6 February 1941. Rewritten 27 March 1945 according to the poet's "Key West II" notebook, where it is referred to as his "first poem," although it is not clear which version is meant.

A variant of 1. 6 was used as epigraph to *In Cold Hell, in Thicket* (1953). Atalanta, the swift-footed Greek maiden renowned for her beauty, was outwitted by her suitor Hippomenes, who dropped three golden apples for her to pick up during the course of their race. In 1. 2, the phrase "the inward tender of her foot" owes to Shakespeare's sonnet 126 (1. 6): "To kiss the tender inward of thy hand." That Olson was aware of the passage, before or after the writing of his poem, is evident from his marginal note on p. 1514 of his copy of Shakespeare's *Complete Works*: "the inward tender of thy love."

Mavrodaphne   ❀

Written ca. 1941. Previously unpublished. An alternative version of "White Horse" (*CP*, 6). Undated TS on unwatermarked paper at CtU. The entire poem is crossed out in red pencil; a start of "Tomorrow (*CP*, 9). verso, along with notes reflecting the German occupation of Czechoslovakia, which had begun in 1938. Although Olson referred to this as one of his earliest poems, along with "Atalanta," exact dating is difficult: another TS, untitled, undated and with minor differences, was sent to the Guggenheim Foundation prior to 6 February 1941 and returned at the poet's request, while what appears to be an original holograph MS occurs in a notebook begun 19 April 1941, although it may simply be an attempt at revision.

Although the poem does contain an allusion to Daphne, the tree-nymph of Greek myth, who as a maiden pursued by Apollo is transformed into a laurel (thus l. 12), "Mavrodaphne" (literally, "black laurel") is a modern Greek sweet red wine (also in Joyce's *Finnegans Wake*, New York, 1939, p. 203, with a similar play on Daphne).

Conqueror

Written ca. 1941. Previously unpublished. Undated TS on unwatermarked paper at CtU; found in folder "1949-8—& back." The title may have been encouraged, however faintly, by Poe's poem, "The Conqueror Worm" (i.e., Death), which ends: "That the play is the tragedy, 'Man,' / And its hero the Conqueror Worm." Cf. also the similarly titled "Conqueror," *CP*, 72 and 73.

Crown of Nails

Written early 1940s. Previously unpublished. Undated TS on unwatermarked paper at CtU; found in folder "1949-8—& back." The source of the quotation, "fabulous formless darkness" (l. 19), has not been discovered.

Mindanao [1]

Written early 1940s. Previously unpublished. Undated TS on unwatermarked paper at CtU; found in folder "1949-8—& back." Revised in red pencil: final line—"that verity!"—crossed out, with period added at end of previous line (present l. 13). Mindanao is the second largest island of the Philippines; pearls are gathered in its waters to the south and west. There is also the Mindanao Deep, a valley in the Pacific Ocean's floor.

Mindanao [2]

An alternative version of the preceding poem: the poet's original text prior to revisions, with the final line restored. Previously unpublished.

No   ✼
   Written early 1940s. Previously unpublished. Undated TS
on unwatermarked paper at CtU; found in folder "1949–8—&
back."

Raphael   ✼
   Written early 1940s. Previously unpublished. Undated TS
on unwatermarked paper at CtU; found in folder "1949–8—&
back." A single revision in pencil: "Negation," l. 12, changed
to "—negation," as here. Raphael is Raphael Sanzio
(1483–1520), the great Italian painter. Lines 9–10 are a variant
of the old English rhyme, "When Adam delved and Eve span
/ Who was then the gentleman?"

Sea Song   ✼
   Written early 1940s. Previously unpublished. Undated TS
on unwatermarked paper at CtU; found in folder "1949–8—&
back."

Who Sings Against Things   ✼
   Written early 1940s. Previously unpublished. Undated car-
bon copy TS on unwatermarked paper at CtU; found in folder
"1949–8—& back." Minor revisions in pencil, incorporated here.

Capricorn   ✼
   Written ca. 1941–1942. Previously unpublished. Undated
TS on unwatermarked paper at CtU, found in folder
"1949–8—& back." New York City addresses in pencil on ver-
so, including those of the "Anti-Nazi League," the St. John's
Guild relief organization, and Raymond Rich, public relations
consultant and chairman of Raymond Rich Associates in New
York until 1943; thus possibly written while Olson was in New
York working for the Common Council for American Unity
(1941–September 1942). Also verso is an undated draft note to
"Ed," possibly Edward Dahlberg, which appears to concern a
loan of money, mentioning "the strain of debt" and Olson's
mother.
   An early zodiac poem; cf. echoes in "The Year Is a Great
Circle or the Year Is a Great Mistake" (*CP*, 439).

Lustrum ❦

Written ca. February 1945. Previously unpublished. An early version of "A Lustrum for You, E.P." (*CP*, 37). Unrevised, undated carbon copy TS at CtU. Dated "1945" on sheet of notes from February 1945. An undated later TS on unwatermarked paper also survives at CtU, folded for mailing and signed "John Little," with the following note typed, probably later (it was originally quoted by Charles Norman in *PM*, 25 November 1945), in the margin: "POUND, HimselF, June, 1945: 'Well, if I ain't worth more alive than dead, that's that. If a man isn't willing to take some risk for his opinion, either his opinions are no good or he's no good." There are also minor revisions (e.g. "Rue de Slave" in l. 33 has been changed to "Paris street") and occasional differences throughout — most notably, the omission of the present l. 17, and "Sligo Willie" substituted for "Galway Willie" (l. 21) and "Aphrodite" for "Venus nate" (l. 35).

This is the "poem on Pound" sent to the *New Republic* in April 1945. Olson wrote Malcolm Cowley, 26 April 1945 (letter in the Newberry Library, Chicago), "I wrote to George Mayberry [assistant editor of *New Republic*] a couple of weeks ago from Key West enclosing a poem on Pound." He goes on to say he is enclosing a copy of the same poem: "I shall be grateful to hear from you and if there is anything afoot I might be able to front for it with the Justice Department. You will understand, therefore, the pseudonym 'John Little.' " The poem had earlier been turned down by the *Nation* (rejection reported in a letter from Freda Krichwey, 13 March 1945).

Booth (l. 7) is John Wilkes Booth (1838–1865), the assassin of Abraham Lincoln, and Villon (l. 15) is the French poet, François Villon (1435–ca. 1463), one of Pound's heroes. Yorick (l. 19) is the royal jester whose skull is discussed in *Hamlet* V.i. Pound's *ABC of Economics* (1933) and *ABC of Reading* (1934) are alluded to in l. 20. "Galway Willie" (l. 21) is William Butler Yeats, after the county in western Ireland (changed, more appropriately in terms of Yeats's actual life, to "Sligo Willie" in the later version). It was Wyndham Lewis, however, in his study "The Revolutionary Simpleton," first published in *The Enemy* for January 1927 and incorporated in his *Time and Western Man* (New York, 1928), p. 38, rather than Yeats who termed Pound a "revolutionary simpleton" (l. 22), as Olson makes clear in "This Is Yeats Speaking," *HU*, p. 101: "I wrote to my wife one time from Rapallo when I had listened to Pound for an afternoon damn usury, expound credit and Major Douglas, talk the totalitarian way, it was as though I were in the presence of one of Wyndham Lewis' revolutionary simpletons" (although Yeats did quote the phrase to Lady Gregory, 1 April 1928, after reading Lewis's book — *The Letters of W. B. Yeats,* ed. Allan Wade, New York, 1955, p. 739).

Olson's address to Pound as the Roman poet Propertius (l. 26) was encouraged by Pound's "Homage to Sextus Propertius." The German poet Heinrich Heine (1797–1856) tells in his *Romanzero* (1851) of "crawling" from his "mattress-grave," as he called it, through the streets of revolutionary Paris in May of 1848 as far as the Louvre to see the Venus de Milo (ll. 33–36). Finally, "fecit" (l. 41), with possible pun on "feces," is Latin for "did."

Lost Aboard U.S.S. "Growler" 🌿

A revised version of "Pacific Lament" (*CP*, 15). Published in *Ferrini & Others,* ed. Vincent Ferrini ([Gloucester, Mass.: Vincent Ferrini, 1953]). Revised sometime between March 1946 (revisions made in Olson's copy of "Pacific Lament" in *Atlantic Monthly* for that date) and March 1950, when sent to Vincent Ferrini.

The submarine "Growler" was reported lost on patrol in the Pacific with all hands, 2 February 1945.

My Father 🌿

Written 4 March 1945. Previously unpublished. Undated TS on Executive Bond, used February–March 1945, at CtU; found in folder "1949-8 — & back." Folded for mailing, with poet's Key West address added at the bottom in ink. Written 4 March 1945 according to notebook "Key West II"; the opening two lines were written at the end of notes from March 2, after a long introspective passage concerning the poet's father. A single revision in pencil: an original "you cheat, death" in l. 30 changed to "death, you cheat," as here.

Olson's father died 31 August 1935 at age 53.

1492–1942

Written ca. 1942–15 March 1945. Previously unpublished. Undated TS on unwatermarked paper at CtU; found in folder "1949–8—& back, " stapled to "Ballad for Americans" (*CP*, 21). The poet's name and Washington address at bottom of sheet; TS folded for mailing, with "Sewanee R[eview]" and "Virginia Q[uarterly]" added by Olson in pencil at top. Presumably composed first in 1942, if title is any indication, but written "finally" 15 March 1945, according to Olson's "Key West II" notebook, where the poem is copied out.

"Fathom five" (l. 13) evokes Shakespeare's chanty "Full Fathom Five" from *The Tempest* (I.ii.397), while "highline" (l. 16) is the Gloucester fishing term for the captain or ship with the highest catch (see *Call Me Ishmael,* p. 12, and *Maximus*, p. 23).

Winter

Written ca. December 1945, by December 8. Previously unpublished. An early version of "The Winter After" (*CP*, 40). Undated TS on Peerless Parchment bond, used ca. October 1945–December 1946, at CtU; found in folder "1949–8—& back." Folded as if for mailing, with the poet's name and Washington address typed at bottom, and minor revisions in pencil. Probably written during the winter of 1945, following the explosion of atomic bombs over Hiroshima and Nagasaki that August. Notebook "Washington Fall 1945 I" indicates it was sent to the *Nation*, 8 December 1945.

She, Thus

A later version of the "She, Thus" in *CP*, 17, written 3 March 1945; revised ca. January–May 1946, definitely by August 25. Previously unpublished. Undated TS on Agawam Bond, used January–May 1946, at CtU; found in folder "1949–8—& back." Folded for mailing, with poet's name and Washington address typed at bottom, and the draft of a note written in pencil at bottom (addressee unknown): "Please plan to play Odysseus for me in a 20 minute's production . . . August 25." Other notes on Pound's *Cantos* and *Guide to Kulchur* verso in ink.

For K.

Written January 1946. Published in *Harper's Bazaar,* 80 (February 1946). Later revised as "Trinacria" (*CP*, 45). An early version, along with notes on Adam Kulikowski from 2 January 1946, appears in Olson's notebook "Washington Fall 1945 II— Spring 1946." Based in part on a drawing by Corrado Cagli entitled "Trinacria" (an early name for Sicily, the "tri-peaked"), but written for Adam H. Kulikowski (1890–1966), Polish emigré, friend of Olson's through the Office of War Information, to which Kulikowski served as a consultant in 1943–1944, and owner of the estate "Enniscorthy" (see "For A.K., Enniscorthy, Keene, Virginia," following). See also Olson's note, "AS OF TROILUS, the Anatomy of Love: biosis," in *The Fiery Hunt,* p. 43: "Diomed must be a Kulikowski: all sword, full sexuality, and what is sensual only the accident of sex" (cf. l. 1).

Lines 3–7, "sown / As teeth, a full armed crop . . . ," allude to the classic Greek hero, specifically Jason, who led the Argonauts on a quest for the Golden Fleece and who—in a story similar to that of Cadmus at Thebes—sowed the teeth of a dragon from which arose a crop of armed men. It is relevant to note, in terms of ll. 11–19—"like a Greek, emboss / The shield with legs . . ."—that in sending a copy of "Trinacria" to Greek-born sculptor Michael Lekakis, ca. July 1949, Olson changed the title to "Triskele," the Greek emblem with three legs (or arms) radiating from a common center—like the shield in Cagli's "Trinacria" drawing.

For A.K., Enniscorthy, Keene, Virginia

Written 4 January 1946. Previously unpublished. TS inscribed "from C.O." and dated "January 4, 1946" at CtU, along with a carbon copy on yellow newsprint. As with the preceding poem, written for Adam H. Kulikowski, at whose "Enniscorthy" home Olson vacationed on several occasions.

John Coles (l. 1) was the original eighteenth-century settler of the place, a native of Enniscorthy, Ireland, who acquired the land prior to 1747 (Olson's notes from May 1945 in his notebook "April, 1945 en route north"). Olson took more elaborate notes concerning Coles and his descendants the following summer in "Field Book—Enniscorthy Summer 1946," writing Pound, 29 July (letter in Lilly Library, Indiana University): "Have also been gathering dope on the family who built and owned this place, and adjoining Tallwood, Estouteville, and Woodville. Started with a John Coles, immigrant from Ireland, Co Wexford." "Lespidesa" (l. 25) is Olson's spelling for the clover "lespedeza."

Auctour 🌼

Written ca. 12 May 1946. Previously unpublished. TS on Agawam Bond (used January–May 1946) at CtU; folded as if for mailing, with note in ink to Ezra Pound dated "Sunday, May 12" [1946]: "Dear E.P.: Will be over Tuesday   Yrs, Charles Olson." Revised or annotated as follows: "The Man of Word" with "Sword" above, added in pencil above "Man of Hate" in l. 1; "Ford" added above "Huffer" (Hueffer was Ford Madox Ford's original surname); and "the" crossed out in ink before "court" in l. 9. An "OK" also appears at the top of the page in pencil, but it is not possible to say in whose hand. Two earlier TSS (incomplete) titled "I Knew Him Thus" on same Agawam Bond at CtU, verso notes on Ronald Duncan's *Journal of a Husbandman* dated 12 May 1946.

The title is Latin, "a promoter, producer, father, progenitor; figure of authority; a model" — root of "author." The "Man of Hate" in l. 1 is Edward Dahlberg. See his "lated tribute" to Ford in *Do These Bones Live* (New York, 1941), p. 30. See also *Charles Olson & Ezra Pound*, p. 79, and Catherine Seelye's note, p. 130. Olson had met Ford through Dahlberg in New York in 1939, shortly before Ford's death, as part of Les Amis de William Carlos Williams and also, possibly, at Ford's apartment at 10 Fifth Avenue. The Society of the Friends of William Carlos Williams was founded by Ford in January 1939 to pay tribute to Williams. It was proposed that the group dine together on the first Tuesday of each month, "and that at such dinners the topics of conversation shall be within loose bounds the works of Mr. Williams and by implication those of any of our brothers of the pen whose want of recognition by press, trade and public is similarly if in differing degree soiling to our shield." See also Pound as well as Olson on Ford, in *Olson & Pound*, pp. 58, 59, 70–71, 85–86, 107 and 108.

For lines 4–6, "the Red" is meant in the sense of physical coloring not politics. See Olson's description of Pound from 24 January 1946 (*Olson & Pound*, p. 59): "Laughing, laughing, full of red-beard, redhead, red tongue laughing." And cf. "GranPa GoodBye," *Olson & Pound*, p. 97: "A propos Ford (F.M.), he said to me once: 'From the intellectual centre, 30 yrs start of me.'" Raftery (l. 8) is Anthony Raftery (1784–1835), the blind Irish poet celebrated by Yeats in "'Death Hath Closed Helen's Eye'" (*Early Poems and Stories,* New York, 1925, pp. 159–70) and "The Bount of Sweden" (*Dramatis Personae . . .* , New York, 1936, pp. 188–89); see also Olson's "'The Present is Prologue,'" *Additional Prose,* p. 39. Ford is termed a "Generous Crotchet" (l. 13) after Thomas Love Peacock's Ebenezer Mac Crotchet, patron of intellectual discussion in *Crotchet Castle* (1831); while l. 14 contains an allusion to Ford's romance, *The Fifth Queen Crowned* (London, 1908), a fictional account of Catherine Howard, consort of Henry VIII.

Of Love

Written 22 June 1946. Previously unpublished. Undated TS on unwatermarked paper at CtU. Poet's name typed at bottom, with address given as "Enniscorthy / Keen, Virgina"; folded as if for mailing (probably the poem rejected by *Harper's,* 18 July 1946, in a letter from Frederick L. Allen). Original version written in "Enniscorthy — June, 1946" notebook, under the date "June 22."

Ladies and Gentlemen, the Center Ring!

Written ca. 4 July 1946. Previously unpublished. An alternative version of "Lalage!" (*CP*, 48). Undated TS carbon copy on white onionskin at CtU, with the poet's name typed at bottom and address "'Enniscorthy' / Keene, Virginia." Begun in notebook "Enniscorthy — June, 1946," under date "July 4th."

For Lalage, see the note to the following poem. Olson had among his papers an article concerning the aerialist entitled "High Priestess of the Circus," clipped from the *National Police Gazette* for August 1946 (folded in such a way it could have been mailed to him, conceivably by Mme. Lalage in response to his poem). Regarding "LE GRAND PLANGE" (l. 4), Jackie Clark, author of the *Police Gazette* article writes: "In the highlight of her act, Lalage knifes her body over at right angles to the ropes. It never fails to make the customers gasp with thrills. This trick—the one arm twist-planche, takes years of training to achieve." *Planche* is French for "board" or "plank"; Olson may have spelled the word as he heard it announced at a performance. Likewise regarding "Einigearmerisenschwunge" (l. 6): *Einig* is "united" and *schwunge* "swing" in German. The word seems to be spelled "einigrarmessessen swunge" in Olson's notebook, probably as he heard it (encouraged by German *einigermassen*, "somewhat"?).

Olson otherwise applies French ballet terms to Lalage's performance: "une porte aux bras" (l. 14) is holding or carrying the arms; "une pointe" (l. 15) is literally "a toe" or, in ballet, poised on toe-tip; "le grand tourner" (l. 15) is "the great turn"; and "fouetté" (l. 16), "whipped" (from *fouetter*, "to whip"), is a turn on one leg, accompanied by a whipping motion of the other.

Lines 18–19 contain a reference to Horace's *Odes*, I, 22, and "le cirque, le rêve de l'homme" (l. 25) is French, "the circus, the dream of man."

Lalage   ❀

Originally written ca. September 1946, but revised later, probably in 1949. Previously unpublished. Undated carbon copy TS on yellow onionskin (used January 1948–November 1950) at CtU, so a later revision of "Lalage!" (*CP*, 48) as well as "Ladies and Gentlemen . . ." (preceding). Probably the version acknowledged in a letter from Lalage to Olson, 26 October 1949. The poet's name and Washington address typed at end, thus prepared after his stay at Enniscorthy, the address on earlier TSS.

In the present TS, the title is followed by an asterisk, with the following note typed at the bottom of the page (revisions in ink here omitted): "It may be necessary to identify Mme Lalage for those who no longer seek entertainment. She first appeared in this country at Clifford Fischer's Casino. She was then, for some years, the high act of Ringling. In Paris, where circus enjoys adult critique, she had the esteem proper to her creation. She began her career at thirteen under the Munich aerialist Wolfgang Roth, since some [*final line missing from carbon copy*]"—all information found in the *Police Gazette* article cited in the previous note, further supporting a later date for this version.

Bromios (l. 24) is a name of Bacchus. See especially Euripides, *The Baccae*—making this poem reminiscent of the chorus of that play ("evoe," l. 40, a traditional Greek cry of celebration). Sparagmos (l. 48) is Greek "a tearing apart," part of the bacchante's ritual (see *Bacchae*, 739).

The Way of the Word
Written ca. September 1946. Previously unpublished. Undated TS at CtU, verso TS of "Bagatto" (*CP*, 50) from ca. September 1946; unrevised. Both an "auspex" (l. 1) and a "HARUSPEX" (l. 3) were ancient Roman augurers; the former divined from the flight and feeding patterns of birds, the latter by means of the entrails of animals.

The Moon
Written ca. September–November 1946. Previously unpublished. An early version of "The Moon Is the Number 18" (*CP*, 201). Undated TS at CtU, typed at the same time as the original version of "Bagatto," written ca. September 1946, and "Canto One Hundred and One" (*CP*, 58) from 22 November 1946. Definitely written fall 1946 (a revised TS of "The Moon Is the Number 18" is dated "fall, 1946 / rewrite jan 8, 1951"), probably in November, the same time as "The Green Man" and "La Torre" (*CP*, 57 and 189). As Olson writes Frances Boldereff, [23] March 1950: "all the tarot poems were written on the good 3 quarter [mile? hour?] walk from the LIB[rary of Congress] here! one fall."

The poem is based on the Tarot card, "La Luna," which is number 18 in the deck.

To Corrado Cagli
Written ca. November–December 1946. Published in *Corrado Cagli* (New York: Knoedler Gallery, 1947). An alternate version of "The Moebius Strip" (*CP*, 54). Another version in *Cagli* (Rome: L'Obelisco Gallery, 1948).

Very likely a response to a particular drawing or painting

by Italian painter Cagli (b. 1910), although exactly which one is not clear from drawings in the Cagli exhibition catalogues where the poem appears or from other available Cagli catalogues and monographs. See, however, Michelle Emmer, "Visual Art and Mathematics: The Moebius Band," *Leonardo,* 13 (1980), p. 109, for a reproduction of an untitled painting of a moebius strip by Cagli from 1947—though without the other figures described in the poem. The "seventh" dimension of l. 16 is probably an allusion to the seventh sphere from which Chaucer's Troilus glances back upon the earth (see *The Fiery Hunt,* pp. xiv–xv). Lucrece (l. 21), or Lucretia, was the wife of Tarquinius, king of Rome. Raped by a nobleman, she told her husband of the deed, and stabbed herself. Her story is told by Livy, Ovid, Chaucer, and Shakespeare in "The Rape of Lucrece."

X to Zebra

Written ca. November–December 1946. Previously unpublished. A later version of "X to the Nth" (*CP,* 56). Undated TS on yellow newsprint (used September–December 1946) at CtU; found in folder "1949-8—& back." "The Nth" of the original title crossed out and "Zebra" substituted (commonly used in codes for the letter Z). Probably dedicated to Frank L. Moore, whom Olson met in the fall of 1946 through painter Corrado Cagli, who also introduced Olson to the Tarot cards and with whom Olson collaborated on *Y & X* (conceivably then, among friends, Olson was "X," Cagli "Y," and Moore "Z"). Moore in his letters referred to himself as "FLM," and Olson addressed him in correspondence that way.

"Steorra" (l. 1) is Old English for "star," while "tresor" (l. 6) is Old French "treasure." The "fool" and "hanged man" (ll. 7–8) are figures from the Tarot deck, as is the "papess" (l. 10). Grave's disease (l. 13) is exophthalmic goiter, familiar to Olson as being what his Aunt Vandla suffered from (*O/C,* V, 22 and n. 12). Actually, it was a midnight early in August 1902 that the Irish writer AE (George Russell) arrived home to find the young James Joyce waiting on his doorstep (ll. 16–17). They sat up talking until four in the morning, during which time Joyce read his poems, to which AE's response, remembered many years later, was: "You have not enough chaos in you to make

181

a world." (See e.g. Richard Ellmann, *James Joyce,* New York, 1959, pp. 102–03.) In l. 17, it is Corrado Cagli who is the "C.C." referred to, living at 1248 Second Avenue in New York in 1946–1947; while the final line contains an echo of Eliot's passage in *The Waste Land,* part I, about Madame Sosostris and her "wicked pack of cards."

Willie Francis and the Electric Chair

Written ca. May 1947. Previously unpublished. An alternate, probably earlier, version of the poem in *CP,* 63. Undated TS on unwatermarked paper at CtU, with minor revisions (e.g. l. 12, "fry" typed over "die"). Apparently written while vacationing at Adam Kulikowski's summer home, since the poet's name is typed with his Enniscorthy address. Folded as if for mailing; an undated rejection notice from People's Songs, Inc., New York, among Olson's papers, with note: "Comments on poetry by Committee   Something should be done on the subject — the issue seems unclear — & drawn out."

The poem is based on news clippings of a widely reported incident; one, among Olson's papers, is an Associated Press release by Elliott Chaze titled "Negro, Who Left Electric Chair Alive, Tells of Facing Death," from an unidentified Richmond, Virginia newspaper from 1946 (dateline July 4), which begins: "Willie Francis says it's 'plum mizzuble' to set in an electric chair. He says you feel 'like you got a mouth full of cold peanut butter, and you see little blue and pink and green speckles, the kind that shines in a rooster's tail.' " The other from *Time,* 19 May 1947, p. 25, reports Francis' final execution the following year (thus providing a probable date for the poem).

"Adamo! Adamo! . . ."

Written ca. 1948–1949. Previously unpublished. Undated TS on 8″ x 10½″ yellow onionskin (used January 1948–November 1950) at CtU, along with three earlier, less complete TSS. Probably unfinished. Earlier holograph MSS, heavily revised, are on Strathmore Bond, used May 1948–March 1949. Most notable of the earlier MSS is one TS that concludes:

That unbegotten day. What had the night done,
the light had taken the night away, the sun the dew
familiar day, yet Adam was not well, had come from sleep
weak, did not command, stand, adore, the night
had sucked his strength away as the sun the wet of earth
as animal animal's blood

Your Witness 🏵

Written ca. January 1948–November 1950. Previously unpublished. Unrevised, undated TS on 8″ x 10½″ yellow onionskin (used January 1948–November 1950) at CtU. The title reflects the fact that Pound had faced the possibility of a trial for treason. The reference in l. 1 to Montana, as Catherine Seelye points out (*O/C*, p. 117), may have its source in a notice of Pound's *Personae* in *Punch*, 23 June 1909, in which Pound is referred to as the "new Montana (U.S.A.) poet," and may have been encouraged by Ford Madox Ford's remark (in *Return to Yesterday*) that Pound was "born in Butte," although it apparently appears here in jest, since it is widely known, at least in America, that Pound was born in Hailey, Idaho.

The rest of the poem is composed of various quotations by or attributed to Pound, as follows: ll. 2–3, from *Jefferson and/or Mussolini* (New York and London, 1936)—hereafter *J/M*—p. xi; ll. 4–6, from *J/M*, p. 49; ll. 7–9, from *J/M*, p. 102; ll10–17, from *J/M*, p. 98; l. 18, from *J/M*, p. 112; l. 19, from Canto 21 (*A Draft of XXX Cantos*, London, 1943, p. 102); ll. 20–26, from *J/M*, pp. 94–95; l. 27, from *J/M*, p. 113; ll. 28–31, from *J/M*, p. 125; ll. 32–37, from *J/M*, p. 95; l. 38, Pound as quoted by Charles Norman, "The Case For and Against Ezra Pound," *PM*, 25 November 1945; ll. 39–40, from *J/M*, p. 112; ll. 41–42, Pound as quoted by Norman in *PM*; ll. 43–46, from *J/M*, p. 91; l. 47, from Canto 46 (*The Fifth Decad of Cantos*, Norfolk, Conn., 1937, p. 25); and ll. 48–49, from *J/M*, p. 128.

À Mirko, Knoedler, 1948 🏵

Written ca. April–June 1948. Previously unpublished. An original version of " 'Elements of clothes . . .' " (*CP*, 74). Holograph MS at CtU, dated only in the title; written in pencil verso a holograph MS of "The Moebius Strip" (*CP,* 54), itself written in ink on a 11″ x 13½″ sheet folded as if to fit in a pocket (with addresses and phone numbers written on another panel of the folded sheet). The poem appears to have been written in response to an exhibition by Mirko Basaldella (b. 1910), Italian-born sculptor and friend of Olson's through Corrado Cagli, who had an exhibit of gouaches and sketches for sculpture at the Knoedler Galleries in New York in April 1948. Lines 6–8 were included in Olson's prose "Notes for a Response to 'A Letter From Italy,' " (written on similar yellow onionskin as " 'Elements of clothes . . .' ") and were also used to conclude "Notes for the Proposition: Man is Prospective" from ca. June 1948, where they may possibly be intended as a separate poem titled "Primordia." They were also included in a postcard to Frances Boldereff, 23 June 1948, also at CtU.

Stravinsky

Originally written April 1948, but probably revised 13 June 1949. Previously unpublished. An alternate version of "Igor Stravinsky" (*CP,* , 75). Unrevised TS dated "xlviii" at CtU, but on Old English Bond (used May–December 1949). An alternate TS of "Igor Stravinsky" at CtU, with slightly different line arrangement, signed "Olson / Wash / April 4, 1948" and revised in pencil throughout with note "rewrote June 13 xlix" added, seems to be the basis for the present version. The TS of "Igor Stravinsky" used for *CP* is signed "Olson / Const[itution] Hall / Wash / April 4, 1948." Olson thus apparently attended an all-Stravinsky program offered by the National Symphony at Constitution Hall that Sunday afternoon, with Stravinsky himself as guest conductor. The program consisted of "Scènes de Ballet," "Symphony in Three Movements," excerpts from *Fire Bird Suite,* and "Divertimento" — which may have some bearing on the poems' imagery. Olson had visited Stravinsky at his home in California earlier, either late 1947 or early 1948.

Northman, What of Yourself?

Written ca. May 1948–March 1949. Previously unpublished. Undated, unrevised TS on Strathmore Bond (used May 1948–March 1949) at CtU; found in folder "1949-8 — & back," with folds as if for mailing. An earlier TS with minor revisions in ink (incorporated in final version) also at CtU, along with another version titled simply "Northman," with minor differences—notably, occasional new line arrangement and lacking punctuation of present version (e.g., l. 8: "is a young man, aged out, title fool"; or ll. 19–20: "In any case / I miss / the meaning of / the show.").

From *Troilus* ❧

Written June–July 1948. Previously unpublished. An alternate version of "Troilus" (*CP*, 76), one more closely linked to its original source in the mask *Troilus* (see *The Fiery Hunt*, pp. xiv–xv, 34–44). Undated and incomplete TS at CtU (no room on page for final two lines in typing, which have been supplied here from *Right Angle* and *Troilus* texts). On Old English Bond, used May–December 1949, and designated "from / TROILUS / (A Mask)" with indication (omitted here) the lines are spoken by Troilus. Another undated TS on Old English Bond has minor differences and ends: "the way, love is / THE WAY!"

Olson's Troilus, more than the hero of Greek legend, is based on the character in Chaucer's *Troilus and Cressida*. He speaks here "as double agent, by indirection commenting on . . . two latter-day lovers at the same time that, in his own mind, he is dwelling on what happened to his own love which Cressida in his mind, betrayed" (*The Fiery Hunt*, p. 41).

Name-Day Night ❧

Written ca. December 1948. Published in *Right Angle*, 3:1 (May [i.e. April] 1949). Original version of the "Name-Day Night" in *CP*, 81. The original holograph MS at CtU, verso a Christmas greeting from Kenneth Rexroth and his wife (a folio of a Rexroth poem from his *The Signature of All Things*, 1948), begins (revealing the fuller setting and meditative quality of the poem in its first writing):

> Night's hour, the outside noises are winter-stilled. . . .
>   Lamp light
> circles intersect, make passage across
> the room's ease ["peace" *crossed out*]
> A woman sews. The cat scratches at the window's ledge.

It is night's hour and once again the wonder grows:
what it is to look into a human eye!
Men, men! What they are who, of a sudden, of a night
in a room not so different than this in which I sit
(and remember) . . .

Four other undated TSS also at CtU, all revised, gradually
evolving away from the holograph original. The earliest ends:

What is it maketh modest man?
But I can no longer on these questions dwell.
I must gather wood.
It will snow tonight, the trains' whistles tell.

James J. Stathes, to whom the poem is dedicated, together
with his wife Cleopatra were friends of the Olsons in
Washington, as were George Pistolas and Stephanos Radis—
Greek immigrants who still practiced the Old World custom of
celebrating one's name day. "These men of Greece" (l. 24) in
the holograph original reads: "these men of Greece / transplanted
to this shore, these city traders."

"who it is who sits . . ." ✿

Written ca. December 1949. Previously unpublished. An
alternate version of "The Babe" (*CP*, 101). Undated TS at CtU,
one of four different on yellow onionskin (used January
1948–November 1950), with alternate ll. 33–34 added in pen-
cil in the margin: "by form, the just act, the act / crying to be
born." For "the howling / Babe" (ll. 5–6), cf. the final lines of
"La Préface" (*CP*, 46); for the "throne of bone . . . mere pea
of bone" (ll. 13–15), cf. "The Praises" (*CP*, 96); and for ll. 18–19,
cf. "The Kingfishers" (*CP*, 86): "if you look . . . long enough
/ as long as it was necessary . . . ," and "the E on the stone
. . . the E / cut so rudely on that oldest stone."

The Advantage ✿

TS dated "1/10/L" at CtU, with note in pencil, "Accent
1/12/50 ?" indicating the poem had been submitted for publica-
tion to (or considered for submission by) that literary journal.
An alternate version to the one sent Monroe Engel, 3 February
1950 (*CP*, 105). An undated TS also survives at CtU, with
holograph revisions in ink.

186

For ll. 11–13, "men spring up on all sides / (like violets . . . ," see also Olson's letter to Robert Creeley, 27 May 1950 (*O/C,* I, 51), "The Story of an Olson, and Bad Thing" (*CP,* 175), and "Apollonius of Tyana" (*HU,* p. 27). Olson's source is H. S. M. Coxeter, *Non-Euclidean Geometry* (Toronto, 1942), p. 10 (quoted in *O/C,* n. I.46). For "act and image . . . a rhythm more than image . . ." (ll. 15–17), cf. perhaps "ABCs (2)" (*CP,* 173): "of rhythm is image / of image is knowing . . ."

"Lady Mimosa! deliver us . . ."

Written 27 March 1950. Previously unpublished. A continuation of "The She-Bear" and "The She-Bear (II)" (*CP,* 129 and 134): the Dictation Bond TS cited below has number "3" added in pencil. Survives in two TSS: the present version on yellow onionskin, undated and revised in ink; another version, also undated, on Fox River Dictation Bond and revised throughout in pencil at a later date, concluding:

> We say abstract,
> we mean, as you did,
> with your hip, form
>
> we too know
> beauty is difficult
>
> We thank you, Mimosa!

A carbon copy of the present version was sent Frances Boldereff, 30 March 1950. In his accompanying letter, Olson explores human sexuality, especially in terms of the Judaeo-Christian tradition, stating: "what i imagine i am getting at, is, NATURE'S reproductions: do we not, really, see her as FEMALE FIGURE ALONE, no fertilizer? and isn't this curious? isn't the Lady the true image of the immaculate, not old White-Beard, the Eunuch? o Lady, the Parthenogenetic . . ." In his letter the next day, he mentions to Boldereff that the poem was "written in one push monday," i.e. March 27. He had written on the 27th when sending her the opening portions: "i stopped to make you copy—and spang, comes the PRAYER! I'll send that too, tho you will see it is rough, new and needs to be polished." In a letter to Monroe Engel, 30 March

1950, Olson also writes: "i am in the midst of another long poem, THE SHE-BEAR."

Lines 32–34 contain an allusion to the Mesopotamian account of Ishtar's (or Inanna's) descent to the underworld, in which the goddess is stripped of her garments and subjected to the deadly gaze of judges. "The Seven you made" (l. 55) are probably the seven Anunnaki or judges of the Sumerian underworld who stare upon the naked Inanna, unless they are the Sumerian heroes, seven "sons of one mother," mentioned in S. N. Kramer, "The Epic of Gilgameš and Its Sumerian Sources," *Journal of the American Oriental Society*, 64 (1944), p. 14. (Seven as a number of heroes is seen also in the Greek "Seven Against Thebes.") "Limicoli" (l. 60) is from limicolous, living in mud (Latin *limus* "mud" and *colere* "to inhabit") — as wasps do. And the expression, "difficult, / beauty / is difficult" (ll. 77–79), derives from Pound's Cantos 74 and 80 of *The Pisan Cantos*. See also "Adamo Me . . ." (*CP*, 182) and *O/C*, I, 27, 93.

For Joe   ✹
TS dated "april 3   L" at CtU. Previously unpublished. Identity of the dedicatee unknown.

A Shadow, Two   ✹
TS dated "May 29 L" at CtU, with occasional holograph revisions (most significantly, in l. 14 "the course" is crossed out and "on each of the doors" substituted). Previously unpublished. The title possibly has reference to Katue Kitasono's poem, "A Shadow," much praised by Olson (see, e.g., *O/C*, I, 37 and 52) and mentioned in his note on Kitasono for *Right Angle*, 3:1 (May 1949). The poem's opening lines will be used again later, slightly revised, to begin "The Cause, the Cause" (*CP*, 190). The phrase is originally Shakespeare's, in *Othello*, V.ii.1. Regarding "the rods and cones of / a pigeon's eye" (ll. 2–3), Olson writes Cid Corman, 21 October 1950 (*Letters for Origin*, p. 10): "For years the best prose I read was not tseliot but in work of selig hecht, clarence graham & other physio-psychologists working on such things as the rods and cones in a pigeon's eye." "Beauty, sd the Bearded Man" (l. 4) is no doubt an allusion to Pound's quotation from Beardsley, "Beauty is difficult" (see note to "Lady

Mimosa!" above). A variation of the lines is used as an epigraph in "The Escaped Cock" (*HU,* p. 124). Fleming (l. 29) is Rudd Fleming (b. 1908), teaching at the University of Maryland and the Institute of Contemporary Art in Washington; a visitor to Pound at St. Elizabeths. The statement (or question) was written to Olson in a letter, 22 February 1950 (at CtU). For "Sound, sd Creeley . . ." (ll. 34–36), see his 24 May 1950 letter to Olson (*O/C,* I, 39) and also Olson's response (I, 50).

De Bono

Written ca. 29 May 1950. Previously unpublished. A subsequent version of "A Shadow, Two." Undated TS at CtU, revised throughout. A two-line final section, designated number "3," crossed out: "And we'll / have 'em."

A Day, /of a Year

TS dated in ink "june 21 '50" at CtU. Previously unpublished. An alternate ending is possible: instead of "Walkin' roun," 'Walkin' on down" ("on down" added in pencil above "roun," though the latter has not been crossed out).

So Gentle

Written ca. 22 June 1950. Previously unpublished. TS sent as part of letter to Robert Creeley, 22 June 1950 (returned by Creeley and now at CtU; see *O/C,* I, 137). An original holograph MS in three drafts also at CtU. Another TS, undated, sent or given to Frank Moore (photocopy supplied editor):

> So gentle
> nobody seems to have paid him personally much mind
> as they did Ben
>
> So gentle
> when he slipped off to Stratford he left no ripple behind
> the Swan

"Ben" (l. 3) is Ben Jonson (1564–1616), who called Shakespeare the "sweet Swan of Avon" in "To the Memory of My Beloved, the Author, Mr. William Shakespeare":

> Sweet Swan of Avon! what a sight it were
> To see thee in our waters yet appear . . .

189

"There are sounds . . ."

Written ca. 24 August–November 1950. Previously unpublished. An alternate version of the poem published in *CP*, 196. There are a total of two TSS and two carbon copies, all undated and each different, at CtU; the version here is a carbon copy on yellow newsprint with corrections in pencil. Another version was sent as a letter to Robert Creeley by November 1950 (see *O/C*, III, 150–53, and photograph before p. 81 there). The poem itself is derived from Olson's 24 August 1950 letter to Creeley (*O/C*, II, 111–13), which is thus the earliest possible date for composition.

Anacostia (l. 22) is a district of Washington, D.C. that includes St. Elizabeths Hospital, where Ezra Pound was incarcerated. For "cleaners" (l. 45), see note to "DEBUNK / by clarities" in later version (following). "New brooms" (l. 47) contains a pun on *Broom,* literary magazine of the early 1920s edited by Harold Loeb and Alfred Kreymborg.

There are sounds . . .

Written ca. 24 August–November 1950. Previously unpublished. A later, revised version of the preceding poem; the only version "titled." Carbon copy TS on yellow onionskin at CtU, revised throughout in red ink, with note at top in blue: "Sent 3 Hands, March 23, 51 — *Mullins*" (Eustace Mullins, one of the editors of the Washington literary magazine, *Three Hands*). Apparently the version mentioned in Creeley's 22 November 1950 letter (*O/C*, IV, 39), thus revisions made by that date. The manifesto of a Poundian group identifying itself as the Cleaners, in *Four Pages,* no. 3 (March 1948), includes as one of its principles: "The function of poetry is to debunk by lucidity" (cf. ll. 39–40).

Signs

TS sent Richard Wirtz Emerson, editor of *Golden Goose,* dated "Sept (Monday) 27 '50 / Wash." (now at CtU). Previously unpublished. An alternate version of *CP*, 200. Another version at CtU titled "Il Diavolo, Il Sole" (Italian, "The Devil, The Sun"). A copy (version unknown) sent Robert Creeley before 28 September 1950 (*O/C*, III, 35). Creeley's remarks suggest the opening image was prompted by smoke from a vast Canadian forest fire blanketing the Northeast at the time as far south as Washington, obscuring a lunar eclipse.

Glyphs ❀

Written ca. 16–21 July 1951. Previously unpublished. Undated, unrevised TS on white onionskin at CtU. Olson writes to Robert Creeley, 22 July 1951: "last night . . . [Ben Shahn] had come up with a 'glyph' for me in return for a verse such i made him last week" (*O/C,* VI, 177), and again, 27 July 1951, concerning "a GLYPH show, Shahn, [Katherine] Litz, & [Lou] Harrison, taking up, somehow, and using, the little verse, on the Negro boy, and the auction show, here, a couple of nights, after, our arrival" (*O/C,* VI, 211). Thus, the poem was writen ca. July 16–21, 1951. Alvin, to whom it is dedicated along with the Shahns, was the nephew of the black cook at Black Mountain College, Malrey Few.

"Hay-foot, Straw-foot" in part II is, according to *The English Dialect Dictionary,* ed. Joseph Wright (London, 1898–1905), V, 808, an obsolete dialectal phrase meaning "in hot haste, without losing a minute" (used also by Olson at the end of a 12 November 1954 essay, "The So-Called Masque," part IV of his unpublished Shakespeare book: "Hey! Hay foot, straw-foot, bring in, the girls!"). At the same time, there is a more distinctly American meaning: Bruce Catton, in *Mr. Lincoln's Army* (Garden City, NY, 1951), p. 26, records that " 'Straw-foot' was the Civil War term for rookie. The idea was that some of the new recruits were of such fantastic greenness that they did not know the left foot from the right and hence could not be taught to keep time properly or to step off on the left foot as all soldiers should. The drill sergeants, in desperation, had finally realized that these green country lads did at least know hay from straw and so had tied wisps of hay to the left foot and straw to the right foot and marched them off to the chant of 'Hay-foot, straw-foot, hay-foot, straw-foot.' " Shiloh (II. 6), then, given the context, would refer to the Civil War battle in Tennessee (1862), rather than the Biblical village.

"as of what's / ahead . . ." ❀

Holograph MS dated "Sept 17 / 1951" at CtU. Previously unpublished. The MS is inscribed "for Duck" (Donald F. Daley, a student at Black Mountain College).

Of the Clouds ❀

Written ca. 1952–1954. Previously unpublished. An alternate version of "The Clouds" (*CP*, 250). Undated TS on unwatermarked paper at CtU, verso early versions of "For a Lady of Whom I Speak" (*CP*, 250) and "To the Algae" (*CP*, 251). Three earlier typed starts on the same page.

The Friend ❀

Written ca. 1952–1957. Previously unpublished. An alternate version of the poem in *CP*, 256. Undated TS on unwatermarked paper at CtU; unrevised except in the act of typing. Written at the same time as "The Civil War" (*CP*, 251), "The Connection" (*CP*, 253), and "War on the Mind in a Time of Love" (*CP*, 258); thus, no earlier than 1952.

Vinal ❀

Carbon copy TS dated "black mt / april / 52" at CtU. Previously unpublished. An alternate version of "Kin" (*CP*, 262). A "vinal," i.e. *uinal*, is a Maya time measurement equal to twenty days (twenty *kin*). The poem is based on a portion of the Maya *Book of Chilam of Chumayel*, as translated and edited by Ralph L. Roys, either from his edition published in 1933 as Carnegie Institution of Washington Publication 438, section on "The Creation of the Uinal," pp. 116–19, or as found in his article, "A Maya Account of the Creation," *American Anthropologist*, n.s., 21 (1920), pp. 360–66.

Black Mt. College—dat ole sphinx—has a Few Words for A Visitor ❀

Written ca. 16 June 1952. Previously unpublished. An alternate version of "Black Mt. College Has a Few Words for a Visitor" (*CP*, 268), dated "june 16 52." Undated, unrevised TS on unwatermarked paper at CtU. Written in response to Paul Goodman's poem, "A Visit to Black Mountain College,

June 1952," collected in *The Lordly Hudson* (New York, 1962), pp. 76–77. Later, in a 1969 interview, Olson was to describe Goodman as "a city man who really would like to cruise cops" (*OLSON: The Journal of the Charles Olson Archives,* no. 8, Fall 1977, p. 101). Huss (l. 7) is Wesley Huss, dramatics teacher and treasurer of Black Mountain College at the time.

Idle Idyll

Written ca. July 1952. Previously unpublished. Undated TS at CtU, originally sent Raymond Souster for his magazine *Contact,* but returned by Souster with his ca. 11 August 1952 letter. A carbon copy and another earlier TS, revised throughout, also at CtU. Originally part of a letter to Robert Creeley, 9 July 1952; a TS sent Creeley with the comment, "made this into something . . . tell me if it works, will ya?" (Washington University Libraries).

A Notice, / for All American Mechanics

TS dated "Aug 11 52" at CtU. Previously unpublished. For "character, / the Drummond light, he sd . . ." (ll. 18–19), see Melville in *The Confidence Man,* Chapt. 44 (Constable ed., p. 318, marked in Olson's copy); quoted also in *Call Me Ishmael,* p. 66, and see Olson's 18 July 1951 letter to Robert Creeley (*O/C,* VI, 155) and "Materials and Weights of Herman Melville" (*HU,* p. 114).

The Picture

Written ca. 1953–1957. Previously unpublished. A later, shortened version of "Dramatis Personae" (*CP,* 276). Undated TS at CtU on Nekoosa Mimeo Bond (same used for "The Collected Poems of," 2 January 1953; *Maximus* letters 26–28, ca. October–November 1953; "West" notes, 4 November 1953; letter to Boris Aronson, 18 January 1954; and "Dogtown Common Blues," ca. 1956). Final lines excised by cutting off the bottom of the sheet. In l. 33, "sail" has been crossed out between "moon" and "stun" ("stuns'l" in "Dramatis Personae"). "Apud / nada" (ll. 35–36) combines the Latin preposition "at, near, by, with" with the Spanish "nothing."

The Eye

Written 2 January 1953. Previously unpublished. Undated and unrevised TS at CtU, on same sheet as "Common Place" (*CP,* 282) dated "bmc jan 2 53" and "The Table" (following). Another TS at CtU, probably earlier, is untitled and undated and also includes lines from what is to be "The Table." The title may be a reference to or a pun on a building at Black Mountain College known as The Eye.

The Table

Written 2 January 1953. Previously unpublished. Undated TS with minor corrections at CtU, on same sheet as "Common Place" and "The Eye" (see preceding note).

Ego Scriptor

Written ca. spring 1953–1954. Previously unpublished. Undated TS verso Black Mountain College letterhead at CtU; found together with an undated earlier version, revised in pencil and on unwatermarked paper, among other materials from spring 1953–1954. The title is Latin, "I, the writer" (coincidentally used by Pound in Canto 76). "Jacopo" (ll. 9 and 22) may here be a traditional address rather than a particular person. (Pound addresses a Jacopo in his *Cantos,* but that is specifically Florentine painter Jacopo del Sellaio, whom he also praises for a vivid description of his dead lady's eyes in "The Picture" and "Of Jacopo del Sellaio," *Personae,* New York, [1949], p. 73.)

For P V himself alone and god bless him

Written ca. August–September 1953. Previously unpublished. Undated TS on yellow newsprint at CtU, with occasional revisions in ink. An original holograph MS (lacking final seven lines) also survives, untitled and undated on unwatermarked paper, revised throughout. Peter Voulkos (b. 1924), potter and later sculptor, taught at Black Mountain College during the summer of 1953; the poem was probably written at that time. Olson wrote Fielding Dawson, 2 September 1953 (photocopy among Dawson's papers at CtU): "Otherwise, it is also bottles: one Peter Voulkos, Helena, Montana. Who turns out to be that potter I sd there was, two yrs ago. . . . it's like a bazaar, Baghdad, to walk in that pot-shop, these days. Great large swelling sides. And tiny openings. Beautiful. And the colors like stones & minerals: he . . . calculates fire. Result: the very damned best, this guy. And a warm man . . . Plays lousy poker. Very damned fine." See also Martin Duberman, *Black Mountain: An Exploration in Community* (New York, 1972), p. 365: "Voulkos apparently intrigued Olson, who took his dark looks and taciturn manner to signify Indian origins—and from that built up an elaborate iconography whereby Voulkos became the personification of the American West and its heritage. Only toward the end of his stay did Voulkos tell Olson that he was a Greek; not at all fazed, Olson promptly restructured his theory, drawing Greco-Indian comparisons of mythic proportions." Little weight need be placed on the story, improbable as it is (Duberman notes its source "must go uncited"), but it does reflect the good feelings between the poet and the potter.

The Feast

Written 29 May 1954. Previously unpublished. An early version of "The Boat" (*CP*, 295). TS at CtU dated only "29th/54," but the following dream note among Olson's papers confirms the month as May (the dream also apparently providing the poem's title):

> May 29th (Election Day. Sat. Also the day i went on to write THE FEAST
>> Norman Ave. And I standing against #4 looking up to 3rd floor of #6, trying to catch Con's attention, who, with Stefan [Wolpe] and Hilda [Morley], and Karen [Weinrib], is roasting, in a deep dish, two cows—who are standing on their feet, no less! Are like turkeys. And for a feast. . . .

The poem itself is based on the report of the discovery of the pharaoh Cheops' solar barge at the Great Pyramid of Giza in May 1954, thus confirming it was written May 29. Revisions throughout the TS are here ignored, since not always clear, although an alternate reading of section I might be as follows:

> sacred sycamore and the odor of cedar wood (the odor
> of the buried boat,

trying to keep up with the day (the sun going as fast as it
does go.

Three-decks. Celestial
food-stuffs. How to voyage
through the night

marvelous Necessity,
who with supreme reason
constrainest all effects

through the night (the same kind of
measures of
the irretrievable, passing (even though they do
—the measurers—repeat themselves
come back

88 pieces of limestone
for a sky, over

—which we walk on, wearing
neither the day nor the night, neither
the past nor the
palpable.

I am slung between stone, and wood

Another TS at CtU is titled "Persona"; undated, it has minor
differences from the present version, most notably the descrip-
tion "the black / idol"—which confirms the allusion in III.17
here as being to Queequeg in *Moby-Dick,* whose idol Yojo is
described by Melville (through Ishmael) as "exactly the color
of a three days' old Congo baby." Still another TS at CtU,
possibly the original, is untitled and likewise has minor
differences from the text printed here.

Olson had a clipping among his papers of Kenneth Love,
"Cheops Treasure, Ship of the Dead, Found at Pyramid," *New
York Times,* 27 May 1954, pp. 1, 4, which reported, e.g., "Linen
ropes were coiled on the deck of sacred sycamore and cedar
wood," although it also specifies that the ship had at least six
decks whereas Olson claims three (six decks repeated again in
the next day's *Times* report, along with eighty-six as the number

of limestone blocks, to Olson's eighty-eight). See also *Maximus,* 401.

The "crocodile" in section II may be symbolic of Chaos, especially since described as another "condition." Chaos as *"the gaping jaws* of the crocodile" is marked in Olson's copy of Liddell and Scott, *A Greek-English Lexicon,* 8th ed. rev. (New York, [1897]), p. 1713. The Diorite and the "towering / figure" at the end of section II are undoubtedly from the Hittite "Song of Ullikummi." See also *Maximus,* 221, and Butterick, *Guide to the Maximus Poems,* pp. 326–27.

For the Children, in the Novel, Mr. Hellman ⚹

Written ca. October 1954. Previously unpublished. Undated TS, on same sheet as "Going from Battle to Battle" (*CP,* 316) and verso a carbon copy of "The Retort" (following), sent Robert Creeley ca. October 1954 (Washington University Libraries). Untitled and undated early TS on yellow newsprint at CtU, found among Olson's papers from 1954. Writer Robert Hellman (1919–1984) taught at Black Mountain in the summer of 1954 and again in 1955; his novel, which he regularly mentions in letters to Olson from 1954–1957, was never published.

The Retort ⚹

Written ca. October 1954, by October 11. Previously unpublished. Undated carbon copy TS sent Robert Creeley, at Washington University Libraries, verso TSS of "Going from Battle to Battle" (*CP,* 316) and "For the Children, in the Novel, Mr. Hellman" (preceding). Undated TS on Chieftain Bond (used December 1953–May 1955) at CtU, with minor differences; sent to Tambimuttu, editor of *Poetry London–New York,* in response to his 20 May 1955 invitation; accepted 17 February 1956, but returned along with "The Bride" (*CP,* 340), 27 February 1958, with comment: "terribly sorry to have kept them so long." Another TS at CtU on yellow newsprint (first page only, through l. 36), with minor differences from the Chieftain Bond TS. The title is listed on notes for a reading at Black Mountain, 11 October 1954, thus date here.

The notochord (l. 1) is a flexible rod of cells; in higher

vertebrates, it forms the supporting axis of the body. The villages, Becket, Massachusetts, in the Berkshires, and Woodstock, New York, in the Catskills (ll. 26–29), are invoked as examples of summer resorts and artists' colonies.

"This is Thoth speaking"   ❀
Written ca. 1955–1957. Previously unpublished. Undated, unrevised TS on unwatermarked 8½" x 5½" sheet at CtU; found among Olson's papers from 1944–1957 together with an earlier TS, undated and untitled, on similar paper (used ca. 1955–1957). The title echoes Olson's "This Is Yeats Speaking" (*HU,* pp. 99–102). Thoth is the ancient Egyptian god of wisdom and writing.

So Help Me   ❀
Written ca. 1955–1958. Previously unpublished. Undated TS on 5½" x 8½" Correct Bond (used in 1955 and again from May 1957 to December 1958) at CtU. On same sheet as "Sut Lovingood" (*CP,* 343).

The Old Physics Restored, or, Newton on Man   ❀
Written ca. June 1955–May 1956. Previously unpublished. An alternate version of "The Seven Songs" (*CP,* 362). Undated TS on Four Star Bond (used June 1955–May 1956) at CtU, along with another undated TS on the same paper. Its opening stanza is the same as the version here, but the middle two stanzas have considerable differences:

> Night! night
> is another business where man can read
> another half of him, where movement,
> and not the moon's—the moon's
> the season of the night as the sun is
> the order of the day—suddenly man looks up
> and across the heavens stars are turning every night
> as each night they go in geometries of motion
> man knows himself possessed of, his skies are permanently
> twisting
> as those are, fixed and unfixed patterns and recurrences
> trysting

198

in him as he would tryst with that self he can complete
    as the tree
—also him—only completes itself by completing. He can,
    himself,
only by the night of this being in which order lies.
                                 History
is what his day is but Urania is the other study
from which the seven sorts of song come. He can make
    his species
total season and see in season sense his own death balks
    him at,
but stars turning upside down in hours, going across to
    and over
the horizon, pulled tropologically as he is in centers of force
and with one wide alley down the center nightly, nightly
    he knows
himself, can there see sets and upsets, Venus gone for weeks,
but she returns in symmetry-asymmetry to fix him as he
    did not know
the North Star does not budge, and anyhow, his poles
are as hers are not as that one only valuable to ships.
    The whole sky,
at night, is book in which he sees himself, with Moon to
    bind him
to his day.

The "seven songs" (ll. 31 and 47) suggests the seven planets or heavenly bodies of ancient astronomy (the sun, the moon, Mercury, Venus, Mars, Jupiter and Saturn), especially since Urania (ll. 30 and 46) is the muse of astronomy. Olson also writes, however, in notes from ca. 1952–1954: "There are seven sorts of song: erotic song, lyric song, tragic song, comic song, and heroic, choral, sacred song. So far as I know there are no others, but the point here is to come back to these distinctions after the loss of them, and to the awareness that these seven are not only what are possible but that they are, essentially, equal across the board, that is, that any one of them is worth a man's possibility, in any one of them, or, if he can do it, in all of them. (It would seem, for example, that it was expected of any Greek poet, Euripides, say, that he should be able to do all of them . . ."

TS dated "nov 55" at CtU. Previously unpublished. Title crossed out in TS, though here retained. Two earlier TSS also at CtU, both undated and titled "A Pre-Existent Poem"; the first dedicated "for you know who," the second "for you." The former ends:

> . . . Bone
> of his mother
> Or at the other end
> of the tunnel: "whee!
> it's me!"
> Bah. Crawl
> back.
> Out in the light
> take a good look, Huk!

(the final reference either to Huck Finn or to Philippine communist guerrillas, active at the time). The second version ends:

> Or at the other end of the tunnel, "Whee!
> It's me!"
> Bah. Crawl
> back
> ****
> out in the light,
> take a good look, honey

The term "mythologem" (l. 3) can be found throughout Jung and Kerenyi's *Essays on a Science of Mythology* (New York, 1949), but some of the definitions of myth elsewhere in the poem (ll. 8-9, "moo-th / os," or ll. 44-45, "lies. Myths / are not that.") are from Jane Ellen Harrison's *Themis* (Cambridge, 1927) and J. A. K. Thomson's *The Art of the Logos* (London, 1935). Section 2 contains an echo of Heraclitus' statement, "Man is estranged from that with which he is most familiar," which serves Olson elsewhere (*Maximus*, 56; *Special View of History* epigraph).

Thoughts of the Time ✹

Holograph MS dated "Sept/56 / the shore" (thus written at Myrtle Beach, S.C., where Olson vacationed 4-22 September 1956) at CtU, along with four other variants. Previously unpublished.

Add an Edda ❦

Written ca. 1957. Previously unpublished. Undated TS at Washington University Libraries, sent Robert Creeley at an unknown date with note: "The author, by the way, is Snorey Stirolson" (a play on Snorri Sturlason, the 13th-century Icelandic author of the prose Edda). Another undated TS on 8½" x 5½" Correct Bond (used May 1957–December 1958) at CtU, with only one difference: "god-head" (l. 3) instead of "godhead"; also, five early TSS on Wausau Bond (used in 1957), found among materials from 1955–1957. "Micklegarth" (l. 8) invokes Midgarth, Old Norse "Middle Earth," the home of human beings. For "Mindinao," i.e. Mindanao, see note above to the earlier poem of that title.

How One Feels About It When It Goes Good ❦

Written ca. September 1957–1959. Previously unpublished. Undated TS with holograph additions at CtU, on sheet of Racerase Bond (used September 1957–May 1962) torn to 5½" x 4¼"; found among Olson's papers from ca. 1958–1959. Slanted line at the end of l. 2 and ll. 3–5 added in pencil to original TS.

Anniversary ❦

Written ca. September 1957–May 1962. Previously unpublished. An alternate version of *CP*, 421. Undated TS on Racerase Bond (used September 1957–May 1962), with minor revisions and a note in pencil crossed out (addressee unknown): "I need a real test run on this one. Please give me your flat sense, does this come off? or is it (which it sure is if it don't) just gross? Terribly hard for me to tell. Need yr quick sense." An undated original holograph MS, verso Black Mountain College stationery, also at CtU.

Walt (l. 4) is the poet Walt Whitman. DeSoto automobiles (l. 5) were manufactured in the United States until 1960. "Kitchen" crossed out before "oil stove" in TS. The Olsons did heat their flat at 28 Fort Square with an oil stove in the kitchen; thus, the boy who paints in l. 9 is probably the poet's own son. "Ontario's shore is blue" (l. 15) is an allusion to Whitman's poem, "By Blue Ontario's Shore," and F Street (l. 18), in Washington,

D.C., is where Whitman worked as a copyist in the Army Paymaster's office (the corner of 15th and F Streets) in 1864.

"future / open . . ." ✿

Written ca. 1958–1959. Previously unpublished. Undated TS on Racerase Bond (used September 1957–May 1962) at CtU; typed verso a start of "A Po-sy, A Po-sy" (*CP*, 107; TS probably being prepared ca. 1958–1959 for the volume of Olson's collected poems eventually published as *The Distances*). Folded as if for mailing. "The" before "future" crossed out in l. 1.

And Now: the World! ✿

Written ca. 17 January 1958. Previously unpublished. Undated TS and carbon copy at CtU, with dedication at end, "For Dan Rice, / Charles Olson." (Rice, a Black Mountain painter, had visited Lerma, Campeche in the Yucatan in 1952, the year following the Olsons.) Another TS sent Raymond Souster, 17 January 1958 ("it's just written, and feels very damn nice"), and returned by Souster with his 2 February 1958 letter. A TS sent Rice acknowledged in his ca. 6 February 1958 letter to Olson. Three additional TSS also survive at CtU, each with different punctuation and other minor differences from the present version.

"Über alles" (ll. 3 and 12), German "over all," is familiar from the phrase, "Deutschland über alles," the title of the German national anthem. "RE- / FRESCOS" (ll. 14–15) is Spanish "refreshments, cool drinks, ices" (Olson speaks of drinking "marignon refrescoes" in his 28 June 1951 letter to Creeley from Lerma — *O/C*, VI, 90). "Re- / fresceria" in other versions. "PUGAR" is possibly the name of the proprietor of the refreshment stand in Lerma, unless it is a misspelling.

How It Was Joseph Altschuler Brought Us Up To Be ✿

Written 14 February 1959. Previously unpublished. The second of two holograph MSS in notebook "1959 / Feb 13th on" at CtU, the first on a page dated "Feb 14th." Joseph A. Altsheler (1862–1919) was an American author of boys' adventure novels. See also *Maximus*, 58 — "Altschuler / taught us how to fight Indians" — and Butterick, *Guide*, pp. 85 and 396, as well as editor's introduction to *The Post Office,* p. x. For the "Hercassian" boar of l. 2 (spelled "Hircassian" in first version), Olson probably has in mind the Erymanthian boar slain by Hercules, confusing it with the Nemean lion that Hercules also, previously, killed and skinned, as well as with "Circassian," after the Black Sea region.

Assuming the Soul Is a Bitch ❦

Written ca. November–December 1959. Previously unpublished. An alternate version of *CP,* 494. Undated TS at CtU, found in letter box "1959 — I," immediately before "The Objects" (*CP,* 499) from 19 January 1960 and shortly after a TS of "The Distances" (*CP,* 491) dated "Oct 15th 1959?" Undated and untitled original holograph MS also at CtU, verso the start of a letter to Robert Creeley from late November 1959, in response to his book, *A Form of Women* (New York, 1959).

A Greeting to a Lord High Canadian Lawyer's Wife ❦

Written ca. May 1960. Previously unpublished. Undated TS in possession of poet and historian Kenneth McRobbie; probably written after Olson's visit to Toronto to read in April–May 1960 and sent with his 9 June 1960 letter to McRobbie. An original holograph MS, also undated, on an 8″ x 5″ sheet, survives at CtU.

Eve, and Lilith and Adam and Pie ❦

Written ca. May 1960. Previously unpublished. Undated TS on yellow newsprint at CtU, found in "Big Box 2" from 1960–1962, pinned to poems including "Compleynt Blossoms April to July" (*CP,* 509) and others from ca. May 1960–April 1961. Also at CtU, a holograph MS in pencil, undated but found with a holograph MS of "A Day's Work, for Toronto" poems (see note to "The Disposition," *CP,* 510 from 3 May 1960, and final lines of "a rivulet of soil . . ." [see below]) on verso.

"a rivulet of soil . . ." ❦

Written ca. May 1960. Previously unpublished. Undated holograph MS in pencil on 8″ x 5″ sheets at CtU; found with holograph MS of "A Day's Work, for Toronto" from 3 May

1960 and another MS verso "Eve, and Lilith and Adam and Pie" (see note above).

The Gleeman Who Flattered You   ❋

TS dated "july 29 / '60" at CtU, with extensive revisions in pencil throughout (e.g., ll. 1–5 and 10 crossed out completely); title changed by Olson from original "Thy Gleeman Who Flattered Thee." Previously unpublished. An alternative version of *CP,* 514; the text here is the original TS disregarding all revisions except the new title. Note at top of TS in pencil: "(as of Jack," i.e. John Hays Hammond, Jr., wealthy inventor and builder of Hammond's Castle" ("the castle" of l. 6) above Norman's Woe reef outside Gloucester.

Thy Gleeman Who Flattered Thee   ❋

Written 29 July 1960. Previously unpublished. A revised version of the preceding poem. Undated TS at CtU on same Racerase Bond and typed at the same time, with additional revisions of ll. 7–11 (incorporated here) made in pencil in the margin. Hammond invented guidance systems for underwater craft, thus "the telephonic hull" (l. 13).

The Intended Angle of Vision   ❋

Originally written 4 August 1959, but revised 8 August 1960. Previously unpublished. A revised version of "The Intended Angle of Vision Is from My Kitchen" (*CP,* 489). Holograph MS at CtU, verso TS of original version, with note: "looked at again & rewritten Aug 8/60!" For Hammond's Castle (l. 1), see note to "The Gleeman Who Flattered You" above; also *Maximus,* passim, and Butterick, *Guide,* pp. 249–250. Stage Head (l. 5) is a rocky bluff projecting into Gloucester's Western Harbor. *"Tsukiyama sansui"* (l. 6) combines the Japanese *tsukiyama,* "mound" or "artificial hill," with *sansui,* "hills and water," "a landscape," also "a place rich in natural beauty." The water in Gloucester Harbor is described as black and gold (l. 9) earlier, in *Maximus,* 6–7.

The Yellow Mask   ❋

TS dated "October 31, 1960" at CtU, with revisions toward

a new version in pencil. Previously unpublished. An early version of "The Yellow of the Mask" (*CP*, 527). Text completely crossed out in TS, probably when a subsequent version prepared. An earlier holograph MS also survives at CtU, with much additional matter: in one line, "in the yellow of the mask" has been crossed out and "in the jack o'lantern" substituted, which together with the date of the poem suggests the yellow mask was inspired by the evening's costumes or decorations.

Another version, not published here, concludes with these lines:

My own self as not divisible
in the yellow mask

A direct downward path
in the yellow mask

In the yellow mask
the ivy people

They come totally
or not at all

in the yellow mask

"a direct downward path . . ."

Written 31 October 1960. Previously unpublished. An untitled, alternate version of "The Yellow Mask" (above) and "The Yellow of the Mask" (*CP*, 527). An undated TS with minor holograph revisions at CtU, on same Racerase Bond as other versions.

The Hustings

Written ca. 10–16 November 1960. Previously unpublished. A later version of "The Hustings" from 10 November 1960 (*CP*, 528), but not yet the final version, completed November 16 (*CP*, 532). The first of two final TSS at CtU, here as originally typed, with pencilled revisions ignored. Originally begun in pencil in the margin of the TS of the November

10 "Hustings"; notes in pencil verso two of the TS sheets are dated *"Wed Nov 16th,"* and Olson himself dates the poem in a note from ca. fall 1964 as follows: "fall 1960 Leroi Jones' The Hustings *November 16th."*

The poet Leroi Jones (later Amiri Baraka) had recently visited revolutionary Cuba (in July and August 1960) and written a report entitled "Cuba Libre," *Evergreen Review,* 4:15 (November–December 1960), pp. 139–59, with a fuller version in *Kulchur,* no. 2 ([Winter] 1960), pp. 54–89. He wrote Olson, 11 September 1960, to tell him briefly but enthusiastically about his visit and to mention the forthcoming report. Olson writes Edward Dorn, 19 March 1965 (letter at CtU): "I in fact wrote a long poem the day Kennedy won addressed to Leroi who seemed then and seems now the 'key' to that very sort of politics which goes way ahead of these obviously transposed events of the sd present." There is no evidence Olson ever sent the poem to Jones, although he writes him, 24 April 1961 (letter at Simon Fraser University Library): ". . . and wot happens when I take my clothes off last night? I knock a pile of papers (mss.) on the floor — & I am staring at my poem to you on Election Day After Afternoon   —by god, I'm going to see again if etc."

Regarding the Soviet Union's "contamination" of the moon (ll. 7–10), the first Soviet rocket landed on the moon in September 1959. Ben Smith (l. 29), b. 1916, former Gloucester city councilman and later U.S. Senator, graduated from Harvard in 1939; as recalled in the *Gloucester Daily Times,* 9 November 1960, p. 12, he was John F. Kennedy's roommate in Winthrop House (where Olson was resident tutor) in 1938–1939. See also "the ponderous Harvard fullback" of *Maximus,* 148. Tally's (l. 32) is a gas station at the edge of Gloucester's West End, near Fort Point where Olson lived, while the Waiting Station (l. 44) was a newspaper and stationery store (as well as bus station) on Main Street, Gloucester. Reference to "longrange / American views" (ll. 72–74) recalls Kennedy's acceptance speech of 10 November 1960 following his victory, in which he pledged to advance "the long-range interests of the United States and the cause of freedom around the world." "Abaissement" (l. 122) is French "lowering," as in the phrase *L'abaissement de mental niveau* ("the lowering of the mental level"), Pierre Janet's term used throughout the writings of C. G. Jung. That "the youth of the world / wears wrist-watches" (ll. 127–29), Olson later writes in a letter to Jones, ca. 1964 (at Simon Fraser University Library), cautioning him that "the power of the Negro is in fact the power of numbers of non-Whites now . . . and the only dreadful corollary is the one you seem not to keep alive, that Soviets and Chinese and Mexicans and Negroes and Whites will all wear watches." Cf. also "*The Vinland Map* Review," *Additional Prose,* p. 62: "like right now poor Chinese poor WESTERN GOODS good Ben-Rus WRIST-WATCHES on RADICAL CHINESE WRISTS . . ."

As for ll. 211–14, "the election of a man I happen / to know / as president / of the United States," Kennedy had been an undergraduate at Harvard while Olson was a tutor in 1937–1938; when asked in 1968 what kind of student Kennedy was, what grade did Olson give him, the poet responded: "a 'gentleman's C.' " Olson wrote his old Wesleyan teacher Wilbert Snow, 28 March 1964, while teaching at Buffalo (letter in Olin Library, Wesleyan University): "the quality of the American undergraduate as well as graduate student is well beyond the same quality of Jack Kennedy for example when he was a student in Howard Mumford Jones' novel course and I was the assistant reading his papers and examinations." Finally, Gerrit Lansing (l. 221) is an American poet living in Gloucester.

Trivittata

TS dated "November 30, 1961" at CtU. Previously unpublished. An earlier untitled TS at CtU, with holograph revisions, begins: "whelk of the water / bore through the shell / of another of your kind," and ends: "attracted . . . to dead things, die / and be all over / the shore." A holograph original, in several workings, in notepad "1961? inside *Nov 29 1961*," also at CtU. The "trivittata" of the title is apparently meant to be a variety of whelk or perhaps some compounding of "trivia." In l. 4, "gelīc" is the Anglo-Saxon root of "like," from *ge-* and *līc* "body," originally meaning "having the same body or shape" (*Webster's Collegiate Dictionary,* 5th ed., Springfield, Mass., 1942, p. 580).

Where They Came From 🌿

TS dated "December 12, 1961" at CtU. Previously unpublished. Original holograph MS also at CtU.

The Osiris Boat 🌿

TS dated "December 15, 1961" at CtU. Previously unpublished. Original holograph MS also at CtU. A reminder of the migration of symbols as well as of the original ancient Near Eastern backgrounds of various Christian saints (St. Nicholas, e.g., our Santa Claus, originally the bishop of Myra in Lycia), with reference to the even earlier myth of the dismemberment of Osiris by his brother Set (see especially Plutarch, "Of Isis and Osiris," section 18; also, Olson to Robert Creeley, 1 December 1951 — *O/C*, VIII, 219 and n. 136).

The Snow 2 🌿

Written ca. 17 December 1961. Previously unpublished. A sequel to "The Snow" (*CP*, 552), dated 17 December 1961. Undated, unrevised TS at CtU.

Kar-cha-ro-donta 🌿

Written ca. 1962–spring 1963. Previously unpublished. Undated and unrevised holograph MS in pencil on 5″ x 8″ half-sheets at CtU; found among materials from 1962–spring 1963. The subject is the birth of Aphrodite from her father's genitals, severed with a jagged sickle by Cronos. The title is a transliteration of the Greek καρχαρόδοντα, "sharp-" or 'jagged-toothed" (see Hesiod, *Theogony*, 1. 180).

Apoptic 🌿

Written ca. April 1962. Previously unpublished. An alternate version of "Examples — for Richard Bridgeman" (*CP*, 555). Undated TS at CtU, verso a holograph MS of "A Short Guide to Present Advantages" (unpublished prose), dated May 1962 in TS. An earlier TS at CtU has the following differences of interest: (ll. 4–5), ". . . otors / like fences to strain off the mucilage and let the / life-giving fluids re-enter the evident? cell we / dance?"; (ll. 8–9), "observing the Phoenician pathways / in Charles' Dish the old lady said get out of the ditch" (also this variant: "observing the uselessness / of poverty, the cracks in Charles' Dish . . . the ditch you will always have with you . . ."); (ll. 15–16), "Signed off as the cushion behind / flew into so many violet bubbles." It is to be noted that "otors" (l. 4) occurs in both versions, as it does in "Examples."

A more precise date for the poem can be had from the fact that Richard "Bridgeman" (actually Bridgman), to whom it is dedicated, was an instructor at Dartmouth College at the time. Olson had met him while giving a reading there the afternoon of 12 April 1962. Bridgman had recently completed a dissertation entitled "The Stylization of Vernacular Elements in American Fiction 1880–1925" (1960) and had no doubt begun revising it for its eventual publication as *The Colloquial Style in America* (New York, 1966) — a subject of natural interest to the poet. In a letter to the editor, 3 November 1983, Bridgman recalls talking with Olson for two or three hours, although he adds: "out of that boisterous, intense conversation, I only retained the urgency with which he urged me to read the work of LeRoi Jones as one version of the speaking voice entering literature."

The title is from the Greek *apopsis,* which, judging from handwritten notes on the TS (" 'Picturization' / via 'View' / skope / apopsis . . ."), Olson encountered while running "landscape" to its Greek roots, through *skope* (see *Maximus,* 296, and Butterick, *Guide,* p. 411). In the entry for ἄποπτος, "seen," in Liddell and Scott's *Greek-English Lexicon,* p. 194, ἀπόψομαι is given as a cognomen, which Olson has underlined in his copy, adding in the margin: "can't find . . . but see: 207 *apopsiis.*" On p. 207 of Liddell and Scott, then, in the margin at the top of the page, he has added: "apoptic — viewed — seen."

"Charles' Dish" (l. 9) is a variant of Charles' Wain, presumably, the constellation Great Bear or Arctos (the she-bear) to the Greeks, identified by them with the nymph Callisto. Line 10 begins with an echo of Christ's words, "the poor always ye have with you" (John XII,8), but ends with the Latin for "to rub" (unless Olson intended *terrere* "to frighten, terrify," or even, given the context, some suggestion of "to tear" or "tore"). "Cosian" (l. 12) presumably relates to the Greek island of Cos, off the coast of Turkey. Among its native sons were the physician Hippocrates, the painter Apelles, and, possibly, the poet Theocritus.

"all covered with feathers . . ."

Written ca. 8 May 1962. Previously unpublished. Untitled, undated TS at CtU, along with an original holograph MS written on the same lined loose-leaf paper at the same time as "Is Black" (see below) and "On the Shore" (*CP,* 556), both dated 8 May 1962. For the "toc" bird, see also *Maximus,* 41, and Butterick, *Guide,* p. 62.

Is Black

TS dated "May 8th 1962" at CtU, along with four holograph MSS, all different. Previously unpublished. The holograph versions, in pencil on the same lined loose-leaf paper as "On the Shore" (*CP,* 556), contain elements of that other poem, indicating both grew out of the same effort.

In an Automotive Store

Holograph MS dated "oct 30th / LXII" at CtU. Previously unpublished. Alternate version of *CP,* 560. One of four complete holograph MSS at CtU, each with differences in language and line arrangement. This one untitled, although three of the four others are titled; the only MS with pages numbered. Derived from a dream, originally recorded (in same ink as the poem) on an envelope postmarked 27 October 1962:

> My mother lying down on the floor entertaining all those visitors (& mentioning that the tourist season, like, & I thinking those very persons are) and quickly I dart a look at her 'parts' not literally but that part of her as, in her position, was also a part of that position — sort of like her hands behind her back and entertaining, mind you, the guests — formally! (And go out then to find myself in that auto parts place in the City where the homely city girl also comes in to do business there (place like a auto parts store or usual stock room) & the girl is 'open,' & I 'skate' (flirt) from the other side of the counter & again nearer (with a counter between us), until the guy comes in to report *the police* want me to report to them, handing me this piece of the car, & I say the (lawyers / doctor?) car is in Conn. & Chas Peter with me when we come out & I have to tear by force him away fr the display of battery-electrical parts this 'salesman' is preparing [for] display, like.

"The nation / is nothing but poetry . . ." ❀

Written 17 November 1962. Previously unpublished. An alternative version of "It is a nation of nothing but poetry . . ." (*CP*, 562). Untitled holograph MS dated "Sat Nov 17th" at CtU, written on notepad pages verso a portion of the original holograph version of "Gravelly Hill" (*Maximus*, 330) from March 1963. A single revision made in the act of writing. Four other holograph MSS also survive at CtU, including that of "It is a nation of nothing but poetry . . . ," dated "November / 1962."

Originally written over the backs of ten Lipton Soup refund coupons from a supermarket display ("Offer expires December 31, 1962") as well as an envelope from poet David Ray postmarked 15 November 1962. Additional notes on other coupons stored in the Ray envelope indicate the poem was prompted by memories of an early acquaintance from Worcester and later Middletown, Conn. — the Ann Denahy of the dedication, whose surname the poet himself is uncertain of (he writes some two dozen variations on the envelope, including Demerest, Demery, Denahee and Demeny, trying to establish it in memory). From the notes, it is apparent she represents the repressions of Irish Catholicism; also, that the streets mentioned in the poem are those in Middletown, where the poet went to college.

The Grain of December ❀

Written ca. 27–30 December 1962. Previously unpublished. Undated TS at CtU, with revisions made in the act of typing (including what appears to be the original date "December" crossed out). Original holograph MS at CtU, in pink notepad between pages dated December 27 and December 30, following " 'there they were . . .' " (*CP*, 569).

"I met my Angel last night . . ." ❀

Written ca. 2 February 1963. Previously unpublished. Alternate version of *CP*, 586. Undated TS on 8″ x 5″ sheets. A holograph MS written in pencil verso a flyer from Olson's 3 September 1962 Hammond Museum reading, with different line arrangement and occasional revisions throughout. Another holograph MS, also at CtU but incomplete, titled "The Angel and the fish."

Based on a dream or a series of dreams, recorded in notes dated "Thurs Jan 31st," "Friday, Feb 1st," and "Sat Feb 2," together with efforts to analyze the dream (e.g., "the fish as symbol of the self cooked right and with the name on the fish & though detachable belonging there"). Reference to the Cinvat Bridge in the *CP* version suggests the "Angel" (l. 1) may be related to the concept of Zoroastrianism and Mazdism whereby the soul is encountered in the form of an angel on the day of judgment. (See *Maximus*, 241 and Butterick, *Guide*, p. 356.) Reservoir Road (l. 2) may be the poet's name for the paved road around either the Babson or Goose Cove reservoirs in Dogtown, Gloucester. The "old friend" of ll. 30–31 is identified in the poet's dream notes as Black Mountain painter, Dan Rice.

"There is a goddess / of earth . . ." ✿

Written ca. March 1963. Previously unpublished. Undated holograph MS at CtU, revised throughout, written in pencil on several 8″ x 5″ notepad sheets found scattered among Olson's papers from early 1963. Opening two lines also written in pencil on an exhibition poster from February–March 1963. Possibly unfinished; five or six additional lines crossed out in MS after l. 205, while the poem apparently continues on a new page with ll. 206ff. until breaking off. Other fragments in pencil on similar sheets not included.

A celebration of the triple-goddess Hecate as she is found in Hesiod's *Theogony,* ll. 411ff. (Evelyn-White trans., New York, 1926, pp. 109–13). March 1963 was a period of intense reading of Hesiod for Olson; see *Maximus*, 326, 330–332, 333–342. Among the more specific references: "the City . . . filled with persons" as an instance of "plenty" (ll. 14ff.), which is derived from the roots of both *polis* and *ploutos* "wealth" (PLE-, PLO-, "full") as found in the "Table of Roots" in Charlton T. Lewis's *Elementary Latin Dictionary* (New York, 1915), p. 947, and used by Olson earlier in his prose "Definitions by Undoings."

"the wild geranium . . ." ✿

Written ca. spring 1963. Previously unpublished. Undated holograph MS at CtU, in pencil on abandoned TS of "Civic Disaster" (*Maximus*, 355) from spring 1963. Written below an earlier draft and enclosed in a circle by the poet to distinguish it. The final two words, "as it"—originally given a separate line, but crossed out and added to the end of l. 4—appear outside the circle, and it might be argued they warrant an alternate version of the poem, one omitting them entirely; however, because of their placement and spacing in relation to the line of the circle, the greater probability is that the words were transferred outside the circle (the only place they would fit) after the circle had been drawn, and thus are to be kept. The poem has similarities to "That great descending light of day . . ." (*Maximus*, 587).

"Planted the fruit skin & all . . ."

TS dated "November 29, 1963" at CtU, Previously unpublished. An earlier TS, untitled and undated but with holograph corrections, also as CtU. Written in Wyoming, N.Y., and reflecting local interest in viticulture and winemaking. Wales Bull (l. 3) is Ephraim W. Bull (1805-1905), originator of the Concord grape.

"Oh! fa-doo: the enormous success of clerks . . ."

Written ca. March 1960. Published in *Matter,* no. 2 (July [i.e. August] 1964), where it is signed "An anonymous contributor from / Wyoming, New York" (where Olson was living at the time). The MS, which apparently is not among editor Robert Kelly's papers at the Poetry Collection, SUNY Buffalo, was acknowledged in Kelly's 12 March 1964 letter at CtU. The passage beginning "myself has seen his demeanor . . ." (ll. 3-7) is from Henry Chettle's preface to his *Kind Herts Dreame* (1592)—quoted e.g. in Frank Harris, *The Man Shakespeare and His Tragic Life-Story* (New York, 1909), p. 373—and is commonly identified as pertaining to Shakespeare. "Oh! the Beauty who had his Heart wrapped in a Woman's Hide!" (l. 8) is a joining of *3 Henry VII,* I.vi.137—"O tiger's heart wrapped in a woman's hide!"—with Robert Greene's variation of the line in his attack on Shakespeare in "A Groatsworth of Wit" (1592): "There is an upstart Crow, beautified in our feathers that, with his tiger's heart wrapt in a player's hide, supposes he is as well able to bombast out a blank verse as the best of you . . ."—also quoted in Harris, p. 372, and mentioned in Olson's notes from Harris, ca. 1948-1949.

Cf. also the final line of "Sans Name" (*CP*, 79).

"You need never fear . . ." 🌿
Written ca. 16 May 1964. Previously unpublished. Undated holograph MS at CtU, in "Notebook started Wyoming June ? 1964—Gl[oucester]—summer 1964," a few pages after a fragment dated "Saturday morning May 16th 1964" in the same red ball-point ink (other notes and fragments, some concerning the abduction of Persephone, in same ink, dated May 13–22). The "cuckoo tipped / Sceptre" (ll. 9–10) is presumably that originally borne by Hades, king of the underworld—or by someone who has lost his bride to Hades.

"Jim Bridger first white man . . ." 🌿
TS dated "June 1964" at CtU. Previously unpublished. Undated holograph MS also at CtU, in Vanity Fair Typewriter Paper pad that includes " 'like a foldout . . .' " (*CP*, 610), dated 6 June 1964.

The fur-trader Bridger, though not actually the first white visitor to what was to become Yellowstone National Park (John Colter, a member of the Lewis and Clark expedition in 1807, was), was certainly among the earliest. He was at least the first white man, as far as is known, to visit the Great Salt Lake, in the fall of 1824.

The poem—while it need not be considered a *Maximus* poem itself—is a further comment on a passage in the early *Maximus* poem, "Maximus, to Gloucester, Sunday, July 19" (*Maximus*, 158):

> . . . caustic
> caked earth of painted
> pools, Yellowstone
>
> Park of holes
> is death the diseased
> presence on us, the spilling lesion
>
> . . . to walk onto it,
> as Jim Bridger the first into it,

it is more true a scabious
field than it is a pretty
meadow

Olson also had written Robert Creeley earlier, 29 November 1951 (*O/C*, VIII, 000): "Cyclops emerges from the pock-holes of old volcanic fissures — as tho Yellowstone had been come on by you & me, instead of by Jim Bridger!" He would also write Edward Dorn, 29 May 1966, concerning "Maximus, to Gloucester, Sunday, July 19" as it appears in *Selected Writings* (letter at CtU):

> —like Jerome Fried, excellent text editor New Directions, had Creeley asking me wasn't it *Jim Clyman* was 1st in to Yellowstone,
> & did my insistence of using Jim Bridger need change! Lovely: of *course* I refused [& happily shortly thereafter read Chas. Peter's Mountain Main — & hadn't in fact run into that wonderful story of Bridger when 1st out there building a cor- acle out of bullhide and branches one morning to go find the outlet of the Bear much to Jim Fitzpatrick['s] concern he should, by himself
> and turned up 5 weeks later saving the huge salt ocean the thing did end up in — [Salt Lake!

Have Them Naked Instead

TS dated "Saturday June 6 LXIV" at CtU. Previously un- published. A companion to " 'like a foldout . . .' " (*CP*, 610). "Have" written in pencil above original "make" of title, "make" not crossed out; however, title given as "Have Them Naked Instead" in the following note on the flyleaf of Mircea Eliade, *Myths, Dreams and Mysteries* (New York, 1960): "Sat. June 6 — wrote . . . today 2 Epimenides (one to Dorn; other Have Them Naked Instead (after noting Leonardo's drawings of children as naked when actually scenes of realism of their play. Why did I get such a projection. Or for Christ's sake to take it *ontogeny does create phylogeny*. I am living the future."

Epimenides (l. 23) was a sixth-century B.C. poet and prophet of Crete. Harrison calls him "the typical medicine man of antiquity" and recounts that "his career begins, in orthodox fashion, with a long magical sleep. He was tending sheep, and turning aside to rest in the shade of a cave he fell asleep; after fifty-seven years he woke, looked for his sheep, met his younger brother, now a grey-haired man, and learnt the truth" (*Themis,* pp. 52–53; Olson underlines the phrase "after fifty-seven years he woke" in his copy, adding an exclamation point). The story is originally told by Diogenes Laertius (C. D. Yonge trans., London, 1891, pp. 50–53).

"Barbara Whirlwind . . ."

Written September of October 1964, after September 18 and before October 9. Previously unpublished. Original holograph MS at CtU, written on a letter to Olson from Marilyn Schimek, English Department secretary at SUNY Buffalo, 18 September 1964. It was written first quickly in pencil—"Barbara Whirlwind / Ital Sandw"—then in red ballpoint: "An Italian / sandwish called [*with arrow drawn to*] Barbara Whirlwind," and again: "*meat*? sandwich / ya / *Italian / Sandwich.*" Possibly dream jottings or similar hastily recorded material; in any case, the lines were then typed twice, on separate sheets, one with a note in blue ball-point ink at the bottom: "(*before* Friday / Oct 9th." The text here differs from the other version only by having its second line typed one pica further right. No further identification of "Barbara Whirlwind" is known.

My Goddess

TS dated "Friday April 16th / 1965" at CtU. Previously unpublished. An original holograph MS also at CtU, verso a page of a carbon copy TS of "The Multiversity   Passages 21" sent by Robert Duncan.

Lovers

TS dated "Aurora / Friday / May 29th / LXV" at CtU. Previously unpublished. "Music in the New Found Land" (l. 6) possibly echoes the title of Wilfrid Mellers' *Music in a New Found Land: Themes and Developments in the History of American Music* (London, 1964), which twice quotes from *The Maximus Poems* for chapter epigraphs and which Olson had read in September 1964.

"These people and their / Amusement Park . . ." ❀

TS dated "November 20th, 1965" at CtU. Previously unpublished. Undated holograph MS also at CtU. David (l. 9) is presumably the Biblical king of Judah and Israel, although no date is traditionally assigned his birthday.

"Melville's sense of blooming late . . ." ❀

TS dated "Saturday January 22 1966" at CtU. Previously unpublished. Two holograph MSS also at CtU. Allusion is made in lines 3–5 to Melville's poem, "After the Pleasure Party."

February 1968 ❀

TS dated "Wednesday, February / 28th" (1968) at CtU. Previously unpublished. "*Only*" crossed out at the beginning of l. 10 in TS ("*only* Muslim"). Two holograph MSS also at CtU, the earliest containing the following passage: "the inner logistics of / Black Nationalism is / revenge / otherwise all is /*only* Muslim . . ."; another passage containing a reference to "Vietnam" crossed out. Giap (l. 8) is Vo Nguyen Giap (b. 1912), the Vietnamese military commander who defeated the Fench at Dien Bien Phu in 1954 and who masterminded victories against American forces at Khe Sanh and in the Tet Offensive in January and February 1968.

❀

Index

Printed January 1989 in Santa Barbara & Ann Arbor
for the Black Sparrow Press by Graham Mackintosh
& Edwards Brothers Inc. Design by Barbara Martin.
This edition is printed in paper wrappers; there
are 300 cloth trade copies; & 126 copies handbound
in boards by Earle Gray have been signed by the
editor.

Photo courtesy Charles Olson Collection. Literary Archives,
University of Connecticut Library.

CHARLES OLSON (1910–1970) was born in Worcester, Massachusetts. He studied at Wesleyan University and Yale University and earned degrees at Harvard University where he taught from 1936 to 1939. As the rector of Black Mountain College, North Carolina during the 1950s he influenced a generation of writers and artists. A seminal figure in post–World War II literature, Olson helped to define postmodern poetics. His poetry is marked by an extraordinary range of interest and depth of feeling in a voice which is at once distinctively American and universal, intimate and yet grand.

GEORGE F. BUTTERICK studied with both Charles Olson and Robert Creeley at the State University of New York at Buffalo, where he received his Ph.D. in 1970. He served as Curator of Literary Archives at the University of Connecticut, until his death in July, 1988. His edition of Charles Olson's *Maximus Poems* won him the National Book Award. The American Book Award was given to his edition of *The Collected Poems of Charles Olson.* His own *Collected Poems* has been published posthumously.